D1121296

Cultivating Engaged Staff

CULTIVATING ENGAGED STAFF

Better Management for Better Libraries

Margaret Zelman Law

An Imprint of ABC-CLIO, LLC
Santa Barbara, California • Denver, Colorado

Copyright © 2017 by Margaret Zelman Law

All rights reserved. No part of this publication may be reproduced, stored in a retrieval system, or transmitted, in any form or by any means, electronic, mechanical, photocopying, recording, or otherwise, except for the inclusion of brief quotations in a review, without prior permission in writing from the publisher.

Library of Congress Cataloging-in-Publication Data

Names: Law, Margaret Zelman, author.
Title: Cultivating engaged staff : better management for better libraries/
    Margaret Zelman Law.
Description: Santa Barbara, California : Libraries Unlimited, an Imprint of
    ABC-CLIO, LLC, [2017] | Includes bibliographical references and index.
Identifiers: LCCN 2017004832 (print) | LCCN 2017039284 (ebook) | ISBN
    9781440852237 (ebook) | ISBN 9781440852220 (paperback : acid-free paper)
Subjects: LCSH: Library personnel management. | Library employees—Attitudes. |
    Library employees—In-service training. | Librarians—Professional
    relationships | Organizational behaviour. | Employee motivation.
Classification: LCC Z682 (ebook) | LCC Z682 .L39 2017 (print) |
    DDC 023—dc23
LC record available at https://lccn.loc.gov/2017004832

ISBN: 978–1–4408–5222–0
EISBN: 978–1–4408–5223–7

21 20 19 18 17   1 2 3 4 5

This book is also available as an eBook.

Libraries Unlimited
An Imprint of ABC-CLIO, LLC

ABC-CLIO, LLC
130 Cremona Drive, P.O. Box 1911
Santa Barbara, California 93116-1911
www.abc-clio.com

This book is printed on acid-free paper ∞

Manufactured in the United States of America

For Michael
1974–2014

Contents

Acknowledgments

It takes a village, or at least a community, to write a book. This book would not have been possible without the support and encouragement of friends and colleagues around the world. Their willingness to discuss practical applications, to share their stories, and to provide feedback have all contributed to the final product. Without the backing of Dr. Kay Devine, of Athabasca University, the research behind this work would never have been completed. My sincere thanks and gratitude.

A more formal thank you to my employer, the University of Alberta Libraries, for granting me a leave in order to write, and to my colleagues there for providing me with endless library service.

It all combines to remind me of one of the most positive aspects of librarianship: the commitment to collaboration.

Introduction: Employees and Their Relationships with Work

Any manager would love to work with engaged colleagues, ready and eager when they come to work, looking ahead to the challenges and rewards of the day. Every manager knows, however, that this is not always what happens. Some days it seems like staff members drag their reluctant bodies to work, leaving their hearts and souls at home. What are the causes of this malaise? In some cases it is a result of individual differences, but much of it is shaped by the working environment.

Part of the enigma employee engagement results from within the individual employee and reflects choices, priorities, and even personality. A larger part rests with the workplace, with the general climate of the organization, with policies and procedures, and with the behavior of different levels of management. This is the part that any manager can influence, and this is the aspect of employee engagement to which managers should pay attention.

Employee disengagement, a sense of reduced passion and energy that individuals bring to work, appears to be an increasingly common experience among North American workers. In the United States alone, it is estimated that disengagement results in the loss of several billion dollars each year in the business and commercial sector as a result of reduced levels of energy applied to work leading to reduced productivity. Similar results have been found in studies worldwide, from such disparate places as Bangladesh, Korea, and Romania. Although library and information organizations do not lose money, they still suffer from the loss of staff energy and enthusiasm. Engagement is defined in many ways, but one of the most widely used definitions is the extent to which an employee is physically, cognitively, and emotionally involved in the performance of his or her job and demonstrates this through energy, dedication, and absorption in the job (González-Romá, Schaufeli, Bakker, & Lloret, 2006). This is the definition that is used throughout this book.

As a result of its impact on productivity and absenteeism, employee engagement has become a major consideration for managers. In a 2014 study, 78% of U.S. business leaders identified engagement as urgent or important to their success, but almost none had developed any strategies to address it or to analyze their organization to discover factors that might have a negative impact on employee engagement. A large-scale study in Great Britain found that only about a third of employees felt actively engaged at work (Galagan, 2015). Clearly, both managers and employees feel that there is a significant proportion of the workforce that is not working to full capacity or reaching their full potential as defined by either managers or employees.

Why does employee engagement matter in library and information environments? The work that is done in this industry is primarily service-based, even as emerging technologies and changing user expectations lead to its evolution. Employees are one of the major assets of every library and information service; they evaluate the needs of the community, they develop and implement services, and they deliver them either face-to-face or through electronic formats. Like any other resource, human resources need to be managed in the most effective way so that they can be productive as well as healthy and committed to their work. Engaged employees make the library or information service more effective and more efficient, resulting in satisfied customers, satisfied managers, and satisfied funders.

EMPLOYEE ENGAGEMENT

Engaged employees are those who bring energy, dedication, and absorption to their work. They are not only physically there but are also intellectually and emotionally involved in their jobs (González-Romá et al., 2006). It includes three separate components: vigor, dedication, and absorption. Vigor refers to high levels of energy that an employee brings to work, resulting in the investment of effort and persistence when things become challenging. Dedication refers to the sense of being highly involved with work, related to feelings of enthusiasm and pride in accomplishments. Absorption is a description of the sense of being completely drawn into an activity so that time passes quickly.

A quick Internet search or a few minutes spent browsing the magazine stands at a local store will show many ways for managers and organizations to increase levels of engagement among employees to an optimal level. Many of these sites and articles, however, confuse employee engagement with other concepts such as job satisfaction, motivation, organizational culture, and mental health. While these are all interrelated, and employee engagement plays a role in all of them, it is necessary to distinguish among them. In order to introduce these ideas so that we can explore their relationship with employee engagement, a number of definitions are provided in this chapter.

While a clear definition of any concept is essential to researchers, it is also useful for managers who are trying to improve working conditions or productivity. The ability to identify the problem or issue that could be improved allows for the direction of energy toward changing conditions that are likely to have an impact and focus efforts on improving the environment. It also allows for the evaluation of the impact of efforts through measurement.

High levels of employee engagement have a positive impact on the workplace. Engaged employees take pride in their work and accomplishments and are willing to expend extra effort on assigned responsibilities and to make voluntary contributions in the workplace. More highly engaged employees report higher levels of job satisfaction as well as the intention to stay with their employer. They bring more innovative ideas and creativity to work (The Corporate Agenda, 2010). They experience less stress and feel better about themselves and the contributions that they are making.

If the concept of employee engagement is more widely understood and managers take responsibility to implement principles of a good workplace environment to nurture and sustain engagement, higher levels of energy and productivity will be made available to library and information workplaces. While this may not always apply to every individual, in general, the organization will benefit from more highly engaged staff members. This is critically important at a time when funding is uncertain and the environment is changing rapidly. The enthusiasm of staff members, their energy for their work, and their commitment to success will help libraries move through these changes and continue to provide high-quality service.

The workplace must evolve to engage the kinds of talented people that libraries and information services need for continued success. Many management books provide excellent advice on developing and implementing improved human resource processes, such as recruitment and appraisal, but the value of these is lost when they are used in an environment that is not itself healthy. A supportive environment that nurtures engagement in employees will provide better outcomes for both the employees and the organization. This does require change in most organizations, ranging from simple adjustments to entirely new ways of thinking about employees.

Increasing levels of autonomy, adapting work processes and expectations, and tailoring jobs to individual needs and interests may seem contrary to the activities of many human resource departments. Clear processes and job descriptions, supported by defined appraisal processes, are the norm in an environment of increased accountability and may be difficult to change. To make this more complicated, there is not one type of environment or work climate that is equally appropriate for everyone. Not all employees are comfortable or thrive in environments that are ambiguous, and their needs for structure and order must also be addressed. To make the changes necessary, more responsibility will rest on supervisors and managers to be adaptive and foster environments where employees are both willing and able to bring their best efforts to the workplace (Marcum, 2013).

HOW PEOPLE RELATE TO THEIR WORK

In order to understand how employee engagement works, one must be aware of the many ways in which employees relate to their work and the terms that describe these relationships. For the purposes of this book, they are:

- Psychological contract
- Professional identity
- Motivation
- Commitment
- Job satisfaction
- Organizational citizenship behavior
- Burnout
- Boredom

Of course, many of these are interwoven and can simultaneously contribute to engagement and be influenced by it. They are also frequently confused, so definitions and brief introductions of each concept follow below. For readers interested in more fully exploring some of these concepts, a list of references is provided at the end of the book.

The Psychological Contract

At the core of how individuals interact with their workplace is the psychological contract, which is distinct from any negotiated or written agreements. Employers frequently observe that employees have expectations about work and their obligations to their employer that are not part of their expectations or any formal documents such as job descriptions of employee handbooks. In 1994, Denise Rousseau, an American researcher, defined the psychological contract as a description for these expectations, and a new way of looking at employer-employee relationships began. She described the psychological contract as a person's beliefs about what is expected of them at work, such as the tasks that they are responsible for and how hard they should be working. Since a contract is an exchange agreement between two parties, the other element is the same person's belief about what the employer owes them in exchange, not just money, but other benefits such as the level of autonomy they expect, opportunities for advancement, or job security. Because these contracts exist entirely in the mind of an individual employee, they are difficult to assess, and it is sometimes unclear who the other party in the agreement is believed to be. In some cases it is their direct supervisor, in some cases the senior management of the organization, and in some cases the organization itself (Rousseau, 1995).

Two characteristics make psychological contracts different from written contracts. First, they are entirely personal. Each person in an organization constructs a different psychological contract, even if they are in the same position with the same employer. One person might believe that the organization owes them opportunities for growth and career advancement, while another expects a high level of autonomy, both in exchange for the same work. This becomes significant when a manager is trying to recognize or reward people in appropriate ways.

One of my colleagues described it to me like this:

> It is interesting how much people are focussing on pay in this economic climate, when there are so many other things provided by this employer. This is a safe working place, and we have regular work in an interesting environment. Compared to people in industry, we have a lot of flexibility to solve problems in different ways.

Although this person may be unaware of the term *psychological contract*, he or she nonetheless expresses a belief in an unwritten exchange agreement with his or her employer. In addition to money, they expect rewards relating to some specific working conditions, and in particular, work that is interesting and flexible.

Other distinguishing characteristics of psychological contracts are that they change very slowly on their own and are difficult to change from the outside. As new information that might affect a psychological contract is received, people are likely to interpret it in ways that support their existing beliefs. Managers are often bewildered and frustrated when a clearly articulated change in management direction is not absorbed by employees. One reason change can fail, despite significant communication efforts, is that it contradicts beliefs about what should happen and is therefore discounted or discarded (Rousseau, 2001). Psychological contracts do grow and evolve over time. The longer someone works for an organization, the greater the number and diversity of perceived obligations, which in turn, increases the complexity of the psychological contract.

Psychological contracts are important for managers to be aware of because there can be serious consequences when they are breached. When individuals believe that management has not lived up to their expectations, they experience a wide array of negative emotions. Because the entire psychological contract is subjective (and unwritten), breaches may occur without any reference to formal employer obligations and often result in emotionally intense reactions. The sense of violation, often described as betrayal, affects attitudes and behavior. Employees who experience a strong sense of injustice resulting from a psychological contract breach may look for ways to restore balance, for example, by decreasing the amount of effort that they put into their work.

When the psychological contract includes a perception of the appropriate level of work due to training or experience, a breach may occur if someone is assigned work that is of a lower status or complexity than they expect. This gap between the expectations of the employees and the reality of their work experience is referred to as "role discrepancy" and has been found to be a particular form of psychological contract breach (Hsiung & Tsai, 2009). In the changing role of librarians, for example, the expectation that librarians will help users with technical problems such as printing may be perceived as work that is not appropriate for their professional status. Conversely, not being allowed to help with technical problems may be interpreted as not allowing an appropriate level of discretion over their work and may conflict with a belief that their job is to provide service to library users.

Numerous articles in library literature identify new roles for librarians, requiring new skills and new ways of working. These include such things as advocacy (e.g., raising awareness of the library's value among stakeholders) and proactivity (e.g., influencing public policy and building partnerships; Schwartz, 2016). Librarians who have structured their work expectations around staying in the library and providing direct service may consider this work to be outside of their psychological contract. Particularly difficult is that many of these new skills, such as creativity, people skills, and critical thinking, are not objectively defined. When managers and staff do not share a mutual understanding of subjective expectations, people are less able to judge their own success in meeting the expectations of others and less sure in judging their own level of competence. The importance of clear communication about expectations cannot be underestimated.

Professional Identity

Professional identity is a measure of how closely individuals identify with their profession and their sense of emotional connection with it. An understanding of professional identity is important in the workplace because it affects the way in which people assess and react to their assigned responsibilities and influences their assessment of whether that work is aligned with their professional values and skills. Individuals with a strong professional identity integrate the attitudes, values, knowledge, and beliefs held by other members of their profession into their views. Those with strong professional identities place a high value on activities that are aligned with their professional skills and may react negatively when asked to do activities that they think are not appropriate, particularly those of a lower skill level.

These beliefs and values begin to develop through the socialization that occurs during professional training and continues to be refined through interaction with others in the workplace and in professional association activities. Professional identity acts as a filter and alters people's interpretation and reaction to responsibilities at work. It is often the source of people's complaints when they are asked to do something that they say is, "Not my job." On the other hand, when work is aligned with an individual's professional identity, the result is a greater level of both job satisfaction and commitment to the employer.

Employees who perceive alignment between their work responsibilities and their personal values, interests, and competencies are more involved with their jobs. Professional identity, therefore, has a role to play in employee engagement and affects the work environment, particularly during periods of rapid change. As professional identity is internal to each individual, it is not something that can be readily managed. Employers may choose, however, to be aware of it during the recruitment process or may choose to develop it through supporting involvement in professional associations and continuing professional development.

Motivation

To be motivated is to be inspired to do something, to feel an urge or a determination to move in a particular direction. In the workplace, the concern with motivation is the level to which employees are moved toward doing their jobs, toward innovation, or toward contributing to the organization's goals and directions. Motivation can vary both in amount and in type and is therefore a somewhat complex idea. Individuals may show a high or low level of motivation to undertake new tasks. The type of motivation may be either intrinsic or extrinsic as they may be driven by either a need to please a supervisor and receive praise or a desire to do something new and challenging. Thus, even a high level of motivation may have either an extrinsic or intrinsic focus.

Extrinsic motivation is driven by rewards that are not part of a person; they come from outside. They can be either positive or negative, for example, doing work in order to get an excellent performance appraisal versus doing the work to avoid a negative response from a supervisor or coworker. Even extrinsically motivated behavior can produce different outcomes, as work can be done with resentment and disinterest or with a level of willingness that demonstrates acceptance that the work is necessary and will result in a desired outcome. Generally, when supervisors or managers talk about motivating employees, they are referring to extrinsic motivation.

Intrinsic motivation is driven by rewards that are internal to a person; they come from inside and are specific to each individual. Doing a particular activity provides a level of satisfaction or challenge that is valued by the person. Internal motivation may be driven by a sense of fun, curiosity, and the desire for new experiences or by a feeling of satisfaction at perfecting a skill. Humans' natural urge to learn and explore appears in childhood, remaining in varying levels throughout a lifetime, and is one of the main factors in intrinsic motivation.

Intrinsic motivation varies greatly among individuals. Not everyone is motivated in the same direction or at the same level. A task one person finds exciting and interesting may be viewed as colorless or pointless by another. In general, however, intrinsic motivation leads people to activities that allow them to develop or demonstrate a level of competence and allow them a level of autonomy (Ryan & Deci, 2000). Intrinsically motivated behaviors come with their own rewards as they create positive emotions. A sense of meaning may come from participating in work that creates value such as helping a student with an assignment. A sense of progress can come from seeing that the work that you are doing is accomplishing a positive outcome, and a sense of competence results from mastering a new skill.

Based on this, it is clear that there is a link between motivation and employee engagement, as employees who are motivated to do their jobs, particularly those with a high level of intrinsic motivation, are more likely to be highly engaged. If they are experiencing a sense of meaning or success, they are more likely to approach their jobs with passion and energy.

Commitment

Commitment, when discussed relative to employment, refers to an individual's relationship with his or her employer and his or her intention to stay with that employer. It is generally described as having three different components: people stay with a job because they want to (affective commitment), because they feel they need to (continuance commitment), or because they feel they ought to (normative commitment). These components can exist independently or in combination.

People who experience affective commitment and enjoy their jobs are often strongly involved with the work of the organization. They feel a personal alignment with the goals of the organization and a sense of personal satisfaction in their contribution to these goals. A high level of affective commitment is linked with employee engagement, as individuals feel that they are working for the right organization because it allows them to do work that is aligned with their values. This results in approaching their work with increased energy and enthusiasm. For example, a librarian who feels a strong sense of the value of reading would experience a level of affective commitment to a library where there was a significant focus on activities intended to increase literacy.

People who experience continuance commitment feel that they need to stay with their job for a reason that is external to their relationship with their employer. These reasons are generally focused on what would be lost if the job was given up and include such things as income, prestige, stability, or benefits. It is often strongly influenced by perceptions of the availability of alternative employment. For example, one of the most frequently cited reasons for librarians staying with part-time jobs is that they provide a higher level of flexibility (e.g., a schedule that accommodates childcare) that would be lost with full-time work. This is an external reason that is not related to their commitment to that job or that organization.

People who experience normative commitment also feel that they ought to stay with the organization because of external factors usually based on expectations of others or social pressure. This pressure can come from family or culture, or from inside the organization, as in the case where the employer has made investments in the employee such as training or professional development (Meyer & Allen, 1991). Normatively committed employees frequently feel a sense of guilt when they think about leaving their jobs resulting from a sense of obligation to the employer, their coworkers, or to customers. In times of economic stress, employees often feel that when they leave, their position will not be refilled, creating additional workload for their coworkers and reduced service for customers. This leads to them feeling an obligation to stay, an expression of normative commitment.

The three components of organizational commitment may occur in many combinations and often interact. They are related to employee engagement in a number of ways. Individuals who feel a high level of affective commitment to an organization generally work hard toward the accomplishment of organizational goals. They are highly involved in the activities of the organization and tend to feel positive about the work that they are doing and value their involvement. This positive relationship with work signifies engaged employees who bring their energy and enthusiasm to work. High levels of continuance or normative commitment may actually lead people to become less engaged, as their reasons for staying with the employer begin to make them feel trapped.

Job Satisfaction

Job satisfaction is described as the level of contentment that people feel at work, in other words, how they like their job. It is a reaction to how a person sees the job and is a combination of circumstances and the individual's internal beliefs and values. As a subject for research, job satisfaction is not very clear, as it has a variety of definitions and measures. It sometimes used to refer to a person's overall feelings about his or her job and at other times about specific parts of it, such as supervision style or benefits.

Research about job satisfaction is ambiguous and introduces many different issues that seem to interact and impact it. For example, people generally report a higher level of satisfaction with their jobs as they get older, and levels of job satisfaction seem to remain consistent over long periods of time, without reference to changes in the workplace. Regardless of issues of definition and measurement, many studies have shown that job satisfaction is positively related to desirable outcomes such as fewer on-the-job accidents, greater productivity, and the tendency to stay longer with the same employer.

There have been numerous studies among librarians, generally concluding that they report a higher level of satisfaction than the average North American worker. This satisfaction has been attributed to their sense of the value of their work and their enjoyment of the work itself. Among librarians, those who have more professional experience and those who work directly with the public report feeling the most satisfied. Most librarians also identified coworkers as a significant source of their job satisfaction (Morgan, 2014). As technology changes the types of work that librarians do and the nature of the workplace, studies of librarian job satisfaction may find changes in the reports of satisfaction.

Employees may go into change resistance mode when their work begins to change. They may perceive that work that they find satisfying will be replaced with the unknown. Methods of implementing change need to address this by involving staff in both defining future services and developing and implementing the change process. While this may seem like a lengthy process, it will eventually save both time and effort by allowing staff to explore new changes and find ways in which they can be successful.

Job satisfaction is positively associated with employee engagement and contributes to higher levels of commitment. Since at least some of the conditions that contribute to job satisfaction are specific to the particular workplace, managers can consider ways to increase satisfaction, such as making sure that employees have the resources that they need to feel successful in their work. Providing regular and frequent feedback in a way that employees both understand and respect also contributes to higher levels of satisfaction (Abu-Shamaa, Al-Rabayah, & Khasawneh, 2015).

Organizational Citizenship Behavior

Organizational citizenship behavior (OCB) describes all of the activities that employees undertake for the good of their employer that are not defined as part of their regular job duties. These could include such things as organizing social events for a team, getting a cup of coffee for a peer, or providing support for a coworker. Anything a person does at work that is over and above the requirements of a formal job description is part of OCB. These activities are clearly unenforceable by management and are a matter of personal choice. Managers can model this behavior, however, and through feedback can make it clear that it is seen positively.

A colleague shared this story:

> In my previous employment, only a chosen few received positive feedback for taking on additional activities. They were, of course, then motivated to continue to behave in this way, while others became more cynical and frustrated. Managers need to be scrupulous about offering feedback, particularly positive feedback, fairly.

OCB is believed to have two distinct components: compliance and altruism. Compliance refers to a person's intention to follow the rules and be a good worker, whereas altruism refers to being helpful toward others. Helpfulness can be directed at individual coworkers, teams, or the organization as a whole (e.g., voluntarily defending the organization in public). It is clear that OCB contributes to the smooth functioning and success of an organization and has been linked with job satisfaction in that satisfied employees are generally more helpful and cooperative (Organ, 1997). However, when these activities become expectations (e.g., speaking out on behalf of the library becomes a job expectation or is otherwise evaluated), they can no longer be considered OCB because they are not discretionary.

OCB is linked with employee engagement in that highly engaged employees are more likely than others to engage in helpful behavior at work and work well in teams (Afacan Findikli, 2015). Factors that support increased levels of OCB include perceptions of fairness, which are also highly linked to employee engagement. Perceptions of leadership style also have a significant effect, with directive and authoritarian leadership reducing levels of OCB. OCB is also positively correlated with job satisfaction: individuals who are satisfied with their work also generally contribute to teams and coworkers over and above formal expectations.

One form of OCB that has a strong positive impact in the workplace, particularly in times of change, is information sharing. This reflects a stronger involvement in team work. During periods of uncertainty, therefore, an organization benefits from management styles that encourage OCB. While there appear to be no specific studies of librarians and OCB, it is likely that high levels of reported librarian job satisfaction found in other studies are correlated with higher levels of OCB.

Burnout

Articles about burnout appeared in the 1970s; it is described as a level of exhaustion combined with a loss of passion for one's work. A feeling of exhaustion is often the first symptom that is described by people. Burnout is more than just exhaustion; it is manifested by people backing away from their work both emotionally and cognitively and appearing to be indifferent or cynical. This may be a safety strategy as people attempt to cope with the level of overload they are experiencing. This "overload" is often caused by too much work combined with social conflict and is particularly evident in industries that provide services to a wide variety of customers (Maslach, Schaufeli, & Leiter, 2001). In some cases, a job with overwhelming demands erodes a person's ability to be successful, or to feel successful, contributing to burnout. Additionally, coping mechanisms such as indifference and cynicism may interfere with the ability to actually be effective, contributing further to burnout. While conflict in the workplace is unavoidable, an organization's unwillingness or inability to deal with it exacerbates burnout.

Burnout has significant negative consequences for both the organization and the individual. At work, employees experiencing burnout are likely to miss work or leave their jobs, as a result of a lower level of commitment. If they stay, they are less productive and less effective, leading to a lower level of job satisfaction and having a negative influence on colleagues. Furthermore, burnout can be contagious when it leads to greater levels of personal conflict and disrupted work routines. At a personal level, burnout is related to substance abuse, anxiety, and depression (Maslach et al., 2001). An individual's professionalism and integrity are undermined by burnout, causing further deterioration in personal and professional identities, with a negative impact on their relationship with their job.

Many of the factors contributing to burnout can be caused or exacerbated by managers. Expecting too much work given the allocated time or other resources available is consistently identified as a significant cause of burnout. Resources, in this case, include not only money and time but also feedback, information, and support from supervisors. From this list, "information," specifically a lack thereof, is strongly linked to increasing role conflict and role ambiguity, both of which are significant contributors to burnout. Role conflict occurs when success at work is undermined by conflicting demands, whereas role ambiguity occurs when there is a lack of clarity about expectations.

Many articles about librarians and burnout suggest that this is an area that should be of concern for a manager. Levels of burnout among academic librarians with teaching responsibilities have been found to be as high as 52%, with some identified causes being repetitiveness, lack of intellectual stimulation or challenge, a hostile audience, feelings of isolation, and lack of feedback (Sheesley, 2001). Clearly some of these factors can be altered by management, in particular feelings of isolation and lack of feedback. Higher levels of autonomy and professionalism also provide positive solutions to repetitiveness.

While library work may not seem as stressful as other occupations, it has stressors that can pile up on an individual and result in burnout. These include negative stereotypes about librarians, time pressures introduced by users, lack of clerical support resulting in blurred occupational lines, recurring reassignment of duties, and constant technological change. A 2006 British study discovered that librarians reported similar levels of stress as firefighters, police, train drivers, and school teachers (Saddiq & Burke, 2006). Among the contributors to their stress level, they identified lack of control over their work and lack of use of their skills.

To create a healthy work environment, supervisors can mitigate some of these stressors by providing sufficient levels of feedback and support and encouraging participation in decision making. In cases where job demands are high, employees do not seem to experience high levels of burnout when the level of job resources, including supervisor support and feedback, is also high (Harwell, 2008).

Boredom

Boredom is a relatively recent phenomenon to be studied in management research. Until recently, it was considered to be a personal problem, with the only relationship to work being attached to jobs that were, by their nature, unstimulating and monotonous (Mael & Jex, 2015). There are significant reasons, however, why both researchers and managers should be paying more attention to both the causes and consequences of bored employees.

It appears that people are experiencing higher levels of boredom than in the past, finding their work to be tedious and draining. Recent studies in Britain and North America suggest that more than half of employees are generally bored at work and describe the feeling as not being engaged with what they are doing. Boredom is understood by researchers to have two dimensions: the duration of the boredom (is it intermittent or is it continuous?) and whether it is restricted to one part of a person's life or to their entire life. For example, someone may be bored by a job some of the time, when doing paperwork or repetitive tasks, but energized by it at other times, or bored by all parts of the work. People who are bored at work may be enthusiastic about their home and family life, or they may find all aspects of their life boring, indicating that there may be something intrinsic about boredom. Boredom that is both related to work and chronic is the antithesis of employee engagement.

Boredom has negative effects on the organization as bored employees engage in destructive behavior or spend their time in nonwork activities. They experience higher levels of dissatisfaction, which may lead to them being less effective, choosing to be absent or leaving for another job. Managers may be able to counteract some workplace boredom by addressing two of the main causes: quantitative or qualitative underload. Quantitative underload occurs when a person does not have enough work to keep him or her busy; qualitative underload occurs when they do not have work that is stimulating or makes enough of a mental demand on them (Mael & Jex, 2015). Time spent doing tasks that seem to have no meaning disrupts an employee's workflow and can also contribute to boredom, particularly when the schedule of those tasks is out of the employee's control.

Boredom may be alleviated by ensuring appropriate workloads and by increasing diversity and challenge in assigned tasks. Feelings of boredom are not always negative, however, as some employees seem to use them as a form of stability in an environment that is changing faster than is comfortable for them (Harju & Hakanen, 2016). Increasing the level of an employee's autonomy has also been shown to reduce boredom.

While boredom and employee engagement are clearly related, there are some significant differences. Engaged employees may identify strongly with their work and still get bored occasionally, particularly if they are not able to complete their work in the way that they think is optimal. Constant interruptions and lack of resources contribute both to boredom and disengagement, but challenging demands such as high expectations can reduce boredom while increasing levels of employee engagement (Harju & Hakanen, 2016).

MOVING AHEAD

So how does a manager navigate the complications of ensuring that organizational goals are met while attending to the needs and differences of employees? Some managers feel that they are already stressed enough without having to be constantly addressing the individual needs of staff members. It is a complicated landscape and can be difficult to find one's way. As early as 1931, articles in popular journals were suggesting that it was management's responsibility to understand the "obscure emotions" (Bingham, 1931) of people at work as well as observing their behavior and the conditions that affected them. The field of industrial psychology has continued to grow since then, with ongoing research, improved measurement, and a better understanding of the impact of the workplace environment.

Seventy-five years later, speakers at a British conference were still talking about management's responsibility to nurture happiness at work as one of the core needs for having a successful organization (Phillips, 2006). If your organization is wasting time and talent by not engaging your employees and creating an environment where they can do their best work, then it is squandering one of its most valuable assets. Even a small number of burned-out or disengaged employees have a negative impact on coworkers, through modeling poor attitudes and behaviors, or by not doing their share of the work and leaving it for others. They may also become involved in activities that are overtly destructive, including resisting change, gossiping, and undermining colleagues and supervisors.

Managers in the not-for-profit sector, including libraries, often have a distinct lack of enthusiasm for business and management books, feeling that the focus on profit as a measure of success is not a good fit with the work that they do. It is true that libraries do not have a profit motive, however, they do need to make good use of the resources that they have in order to meet their goals. One of these resources, and in fact one of the areas that requires the most investment, is the talent and energy contributed by staff members. While there is a lack of critical management research in the library and information field, findings in other areas, particularly in not-for-profit organizations, are readily adaptable.

The question of whether a corporate approach to library management is appropriate is not a new one and is frequently debated in the literature. While it is not the question to be debated in this book, the book is written with the assumption that the library and information community has things to learn from the management research and that the findings in corporate settings can be adapted to libraries and information services. This book takes that approach, referring to the management literature and combining it with examples and stories from libraries.

Library and information services are facing a new level of challenge: technology is not only changing the way that information is being packaged and provided, but it is also changing the way in which people look for and use it. Economic pressures and increased competition from businesses are resulting in changing services and new funder requirements for accountability and reporting are changing the way in which services are evaluated. The result of these changes is an increased need to balance new opportunities with traditional services. These changes all require innovation, not just in providing new services but in managing organizations as well.

This innovation must be supported by evolving strategies for managing staff, for ensuring that they are able to contribute fully to the directions of the organization and that they are committed to the organization's goals. Their contributions are vital to the success of the organization, and the time and effort committed to them will be realized in organizational successes, enhanced services to customers, and healthy and fulfilled staff members.

OUTLINE

This book will help the busy manager to consider issues of the workplace environment that will nurture employees while accomplishing the goals of the unit or the organization. It provides opportunities for small steps that can lead to big changes with more satisfied, motivated, and engaged employees.

Any change can cause discomfort. Each of us has a need to understand how our lives will be influenced by change. While this book is advocating a change in the way in which managers interact with employees, it suggests small steps that eventually add up to a new workplace climate. Discomfort is a natural response to transition, and we all fear the loss of a comfortable situation and experience a level of anxiety about the unknown. A lot of the changes discussed will seem familiar as common sense, and all managers will find ways to implement steps that are relevant to their situations.

Chapter 1 begins with a review of the research literature and a discussion of why it is so confusing. Most of it comes from outside of the library and information environment, and translations and comparisons will help relate it to this community.

Chapter 2 introduces the concept of organizational justice and how it sets the stage for other management and supervision practices. Organizational justice is a major component of a healthy workplace climate.

Chapter 3 provides practical strategies for increasing employee engagement and reducing burnout, with examples.

Chapter 4 provides more practical strategies, this time focusing on motivation, OCB, and job commitment.

Chapter 5 introduces the importance of integrating these strategies into all management and supervisory activities, including recruitment, professional development, and performance management.

Chapter 6 moves out of the workplace and discusses employee engagement as an issue of interest to library and information schools, professional associations, and unions or faculty associations.

Chapter 7 discusses some ways to determine what changes need to be made in your organization, and how to get started.

Chapters include questions that may be used for personal reflection. Alternatively, they may be used to prompt discussions with staff members or as activities for students in management classes. Throughout the book there are stories shared with me by colleagues. As they have asked to remain anonymous, they are all referred to as "my colleague."

1

Theoretical Foundations

While there is a great deal of research into the various relationships that individuals have with their workplaces, little of it examines library and information work environments. This chapter reviews the current research and practitioner literature and relates it to the work that is done in libraries and other information environments. The literature can be confusing to the new reader as many of the terms used in research are also used in more general ways in conversation, and a level of precision is missing. This summary is meant to inform managers; for those who want to read more in depth, a list of references is included at the end of the book.

WORKPLACE CLIMATE

While there is great deal of literature to inform managers about human resource management that addresses good processes for carrying out the tasks that are required of them, such as performance appraisals, interviewing, and writing job descriptions, there is considerably less that addresses the environment that underlies good process. Just as you cannot build a house without a stable foundation, the best processes will not bring the desired results if they are laid on top of an uneasy workplace climate. For practitioners, this is more difficult to address, as it is both harder to manage and harder to assess than questions of good processes.

Workplace climate has been defined as the properties of a workplace, as observed by the workforce, that influence their behavior and therefore also affect their job performance. It is also known as organizational or corporate climate. These properties include organizational structure, standards of accountability and behavior, amount and direction of communication, and leader behavior. As with many of the issues related to employer-employee relationships, the major concern here is not with what the organization thinks it is doing but what the employees observe it to be doing.

One of the most striking findings in studies of organizational climate is the gap between the perceptions of senior managers and employees. There is a significant difference between what companies think they are providing for their employees and what employees perceive that they are receiving, in such areas as training, evaluation, and involvement in decision making (Gray, 2007). Senior management also tends to believe that organizational change results in many benefits, including flexibility and employee participation in decision making, while employees report loss of knowledge and key skills.

Workplace climate is important to monitor because of its demonstrated relationship with a number of desirable outcomes, including customer satisfaction, productivity, and success in achieving organizational goals (Carr, Schmidt, Ford, & DeShon, 2003). It is also linked with profit, which is not of particular interest to library and information organizations; however, the other outcomes are congruent with the work in this environment.

Some of the factors that influence the workplace climate are communication, the behavior of managers, whether or not the values of the workplace are modeled by leaders, norms about how people treat each other, and the level of flexibility and restriction expressed by both written policies and unwritten rules. Climate is the sum of common perceptions of things that happen in the workplace, including both actual behavior and documented structures such as policies and procedures.

Workplace climate is often confused with workplace culture. Workplace climate is made up of shared perceptions about policies, practices, and procedures and employees' perceptions of them. It includes their observations about what behavior is modeled by managers and what behavior gets rewarded. Workplace culture, on the other hand, is the shared values and beliefs that are introduced to new employees as the proper way to behave and are transmitted through stories, traditions, and metaphors (Schneider, Ehrhart, & Macey, 2013). Perhaps the simplest way of separating them is to consider that climate is the sum of what the organization does, and culture is the sum of what the organization is.

Neither the popular literature nor practicing managers make a clear distinction between organizational climate and culture. They tend to refer to organizational culture when discussing any of the issues of either culture or climate. This may be because it is the implementation of policies and procedures and behaviors that are rewarded and expected, that is, the organizational climate that helps to create the framework and values of organizational culture. Most managers understand that they have limited influence on the organizational culture as it incorporates so many internal issues and is affected by larger economic and social forces as well as national culture. They can, however, have a significant impact on organizational climate through their own practices of communication and interaction with people.

The most significant features of organizational climate are supervisory support, performance feedback, clarity of organizational goals, autonomy, and the opportunity to participate in decision making. These are all affected by management behavior. Support from managers and feedback on performance increase the level of employees' confidence in performing their responsibilities and increase both productivity and organizational citizenship behavior (Randhawa & Kaur, 2015). A high level of support also gives employees an overall positive impression of the organization and helps them to adopt the goals and values of the organization. Frequent feedback on performance also results in employees feeling a sense of ownership, both about their jobs and about the outcome of their work. Managers can supplement the formal performance management system with sincere and direct feedback.

Clear organizational goals that are communicated to all employees are an important component of organizational climate. Clear goals support effective performance, particularly when individual employees understand how their work contributes to the achievement of organizational goals. This clarity helps to reduce role ambiguity and role conflict, which have been shown to contribute to stress and burnout (Randhawa & Kaur, 2015). Higher levels of autonomy have been shown to have a direct link with employees' willingness to work hard. It increases the level of trust that the employee has in the organization and has a direct result on motivation.

A higher level of participation in decision making is one of the features of an organizational climate that has a positive effect both on the level of employees' focus on job responsibilities and on contributing to the organization over and above their assigned roles. This has an ever-greater effect when the decision making is in an area that is directly related to their work (Randhawa & Kaur, 2015).

Like many of the other ideas discussed in this book, the experience of organizational climate is highly subjective. It is an individual and personal experience that is a result of the interaction of an individual's preferences and beliefs and the measurable and observable characteristics of the organization (Gray, 2007, p. 5). Organizational climate is to be found in the answer to the question, "What does it feel like to work here?" Clearly the answers will vary. For example, perceptions of the organizational climate vary considerably, depending on where someone sits in the organizational hierarchy (Hellriegel & Slocum, 1974).

The intersection of organizational culture and climate provides a broader perspective for understanding the experiences that employees have at work. Together, they address employees' understanding of how the organization works, that is, its climate, as well as their beliefs about the value of the organization, that is, its culture. The processes are an attempt by management to result in behaviors that will lead to the accomplishment of organizational goals, and the culture is the result of these tangibles combined with intangibles such as norms and values.

THE PSYCHOLOGICAL CONTRACT

An American researcher, Denise Rousseau (1995), first described the psychological contract as a way of understanding employees' expectations about their workplace. She defined it as a mental model that is based on perceived promises and obligations in the relationship between an employee and his or her employer. It is a model that is both stable and enduring and is an entirely personal perception that may not be aligned with other, overt contracts or agreements. The components of the psychological contract vary among individuals but generally include beliefs about how a person should behave, how hard he or she has to work, and what work is to be done. In exchange, the contract includes what is expected from the employer. These expectations are often not monetary and include such things as the amount of autonomy, what kinds of work should be assigned, or expectations for advancement (Rousseau, 2003).

The psychological contract poses many challenges for managers. In a written contract, great care is taken to define and agree upon all of the terms. Even with all of this preparation, in times of disagreement, lawyers are generally involved to try to determine who failed to deliver in line with the agreed-upon conditions. A psychological contract, however, has none of the definition and agreement of a written contract. The terms are entirely subjective, so there is a great deal of potential for a perception that the other party has failed to live up to their commitment.

Research into the impact of psychological contracts is primarily focused on what happens when the contract is broken. This is referred to as a breach of the psychological contract and occurs when an employee believes that the anticipated obligations of the employer have not been fulfilled. For example, an employee whose psychological contract leads him or her to expect that all internal applications for jobs will be given priority will experience a breach if he or she applies for a job and it is filled from outside the organization. Because the psychological contract is subjective, the employer may have never made this commitment or even be aware that an employee believes that it should happen.

A breach in the psychological contract has many negative outcomes for the individual and for the employer. The employee experiences a significant emotional impact, which has been described as feeling violated, accompanied by a sense that he or she has been betrayed by the employer. This is clearly greater than a simple sense of disappointment. The resulting sense of injustice often leads to anger at the employer. This can then lead to negative consequences for the organization, as the employees may begin to act in ways that will redress the balance. This could be by reducing the amount of effort that they put into their jobs or reducing their contribution to other workplace activities. Employees also frequently reduce their overall support for the organization, including such things as speaking positively about the organization in public, volunteering on behalf of the organization, or making financial contributions. One of the unintended consequences of this behavior is that it has a tendency to spill over, that is, to spread to coworkers who are negatively affected by incivility or even general unfriendliness. Negative moods not only spread to coworkers but also can affect interactions with others, including family members and customers.

One of the frequent contributors to the breach of psychological contracts is a belief that the work that is assigned to an employee is not what he or she expected. This is particularly true when people have special training to do a job. For example, librarians who are expected to provide circulation or technical support to users may feel that this work is not what they were trained to do when they became librarians and experience a sense of betrayal by their employers. It is useful to remember that because the entire experience is subjective, a psychological contract breach can occur without any objective failure of a formal commitment.

While there is virtually no research that specifically investigates the psychological contracts of librarians, there are studies of librarians' expectations comparing them to the reality of their work. For example, a recent study (McAbee & Graham, 2005) discusses the challenges faced when a library introduced a different model for providing reference services, resulting in additional responsibilities for the librarians. These new responsibilities were perceived as taking time away from the work that they believed was important. This difficulty arose in spite of a change in the way in which librarian jobs have been advertised over time, with jobs becoming increasingly more "expansive and complex" (Lynch & Smith, 2001) and the generally changing nature of reference services as a result of changing financial support for libraries, reductions in staffing, and the rapidly changing information environment. The resistance of some staff, combined with "disgruntlement" (McAbee & Graham, 2005), suggests that a breach of the psychological contract has occurred. Some of these problems could have been avoided by consulting the librarians or giving them responsibility for the new service model.

A colleague shared this story:

> I was co-leader of strategic planning for combined library and IT research and teaching support services. The strategic planning process helped librarians, who were previously throwing temper tantrums about changing services, to have time to think it through and understand that user input was important and that what mattered were the services, rather than the locations where services were provided. We as a group were given the responsibility for working on campus to find the right direction and then go there.

Dealing with psychological contracts creates some significant challenges for managers. In a legal contract, the terms are clearly defined and negotiated between the parties. A significant amount of effort goes into ensuring that both parties define the terms in the same way. In spite of all the effort that goes into making them precise, there is considerable work for lawyers in interpreting them when things do not work. Psychological contracts have the potential to be much more taxing. They are personal and based entirely on an individual's perceptions, which are strongly influenced by their values, their family background, their previous work experience, and other forces. That means that every employee has a slightly different belief about what he or she owes the employer and what the employer owes him or her. Two different people, working in similar jobs for the same employer, can have very different expectations (Gray, 2007, p. 21).

The other challenge is that psychological contracts change very slowly. Every manager has experienced a level of frustration when a change in management style or direction appears to be ignored by employees. This is a result of the tendency for everyone to interpret new information in a way that supports and reinforces their existing beliefs. If a change does not align with an individual's psychological contract, he or she may simply ignore it or discount its importance (Rousseau, 1995).

Professional staff members bring a particular set of expectations to the workplace that is partially defined by their profession. In addition to their personal values, they have a set of beliefs and values that are integrated with the specific knowledge of their profession. For example, studies with nurses show that they have an expectation that their supervisors will protect them as much as possible from organizational issues and demands so that they can focus on their professional work (Brunetto, Shacklock, Teo, & Farr-Wharton, 2014). They also expect more power to control their work and a higher level of autonomy as a result of their professional standing. These and similar expectations are woven into their psychological contracts and are affected by their professional socialization through their original training and their interactions with other nurses.

Psychological contracts do change and evolve but slowly and over a period of time. As result of continuous input, employees who have been with one employer for a longer period of time have a greater number of beliefs about perceived obligations. Not only do they have more expectations, but these expectations are increasingly diverse and complex as well. In other words, more senior employees have greater expectations, both of themselves and of their employers, than do new hires as a result of their interpretation of new information over a period of time.

The psychological contract will be referred to again in the discussion about strategies for managers in improving the workplace climate. An awareness of the structure of employees' beliefs and efforts to ensure that their expectations are aligned with the organization's structure will result in positive benefits for both the employee and the library.

EMPLOYEE ENGAGEMENT

Employee engagement appears to be ambiguous as it is used in many different ways in the research and popular literature. It originally appeared as a "folk theory" (Macey & Schneider, 2008) before anyone started to research it. It is often not clearly defined in the practitioner literature or by consultants, leading to a level of confusion. Everyone agrees, however, that it is a positive thing to have in an employee.

The most commonly used definition in the research and the one that will be used in this book is that employee engagement is the extent to which an employee is physically, cognitively, and emotionally involved in the performance of his or her job and demonstrates this involvement through energy, dedication, and absorption in his or her work (González-Romá, Schaufeli, Bakker, & Lloret, 2006). In other words, as well as bringing his or her body to work, an employee brings his or her passion, energy, and enthusiasm. Employee engagement is observable through the person's behavior; he or she seems to be fully there, integrated and focused on the performance of his or her job and connected to his or her work and coworkers. Engaged employees demonstrate a positive attitude toward their employer, pride in their work, belief in the services of the organization, and an understanding of the bigger picture, resulting in a willingness to go beyond basic job requirements (Gray, 2007). It has been described as investing their hands, head, and heart in their employment (Rich, Lepine, & Crawford, 2010). Unlike other descriptions of employees, engagement goes beyond the application of physical or cognitive effort.

Engagement is often confused with other relationships between an employee and his or her work, such as commitment. Commitment reflects an intention to stay with the organization, whereas engagement refers to the level of positive emotion that an employee experiences while doing his or her job and generally includes a willingness to expend extra effort on his or her work for the success of the organization.

Both organizations and individuals benefit from a high level of engagement. Highly engaged individuals report high levels of energy, good health, and a strong identification with their work. These lead to benefits for the organization, including high levels of organization citizenship behavior, such as, volunteering to take on additional responsibilities for nonwork activities like organizing social events. High levels of engagement have been linked with job satisfaction, intention to stay with one employer, and higher levels of customer satisfaction. In the same way that negative emotions affect coworkers, positive ones also have a spillover effect and contribute to an improvement in the overall work environment.

Employee engagement is also discussed by using the term *disengagement*, which refers to the loss of passion and energy about work. This is also a term that is used loosely, as there seems to be no definition about how much reduction in engagement leads to disengagement. When people begin a job, they are typically fully engaged, excited about the opportunities ahead, with high levels of enthusiasm. They are eager to do their jobs and are ready to commit time and energy to being successful. The challenge for managers is to create an environment where employees can continue with this level of engagement, with the resulting benefits for both the employee and the organization.

Interest in the research literature about the conditions that promote employee engagement is increasing. They include such diverse factors as positive and effective relationships with managers and coworkers, interesting and worthwhile work, and sufficient resources to do the job (Brunetto et al., 2014). One of the most significant antecedents of employee engagement is referred to as meaningfulness. This refers to an experience that employees have that their work is useful and valuable and aligned with their own values. Employees who find that when their work matches the way they like to see themselves, they are typically more engaged (Rich et al., 2010). Thus, a library employee who sees himself or herself as being a helpful person will feel more engaged in a role where he or she is able to be helpful to others. Conversely, an employee who prefers to see himself or herself as analytical may find public service to be less engaging than resolving technical problems. Employees who are assigned work that they feel is inappropriate for their self-image report feeling taken advantage of and therefore less willing to engage fully with their jobs. It is possible to see the role of the psychological contract in this sense, if employees expect their employers to provide work that is meaningful for them.

One of the other conditions supporting a high level of employee engagement is perceived organizational support. Employees feel free to fully engage themselves in their work when they believe that they have a high level of predictable and clear support from their organization and from their supervisor, and they have authentic interpersonal relationships with others. This creates a setting where they feel safely able to take risks and to express themselves at work. People typically feel safer when they have some level of control over their work and often interpret management's reluctance to allow a level of autonomy as a message that they are not to be trusted and that there will be negative consequences to overstepping boundaries. When employees feel that they have a high level of organizational support, they are not concerned about potential negative effects of engaging fully with their work. On the contrary, when they perceive that organizational support is lacking, they may choose to keep their heads down and disengage rather than risk negative repercussions (Rich et al., 2010).

While there is virtually no research about workplace engagement and librarians, findings from other areas can lead us to some conclusions about issues affecting librarians' engagement. For example, there are several studies of engagement in nursing that might be comparable to librarianship, as it is exposed to similar stresses of funding, technological change, and changing work expectations.

For example, a study of British nurses found that a lack of time to do their jobs in the way that they wanted to and to establish positive connections with patients combined with a lack of autonomy and a feeling that their work was no longer meaningful were related to reduced levels of engagement. This disengagement affected their relationships both with their employer and with nursing in general. Role ambiguity, that is, a lack of clarity about expectations in the workplace, was also found to result in a growing level of disengagement (Carter & Tourangeau, 2012). This is not unlike the situation in which some librarians find themselves as their work shifts away from direct contact with library users, and they begin to question whether their new roles have meaning. Role ambiguity is very likely to occur in organizations or professions that are undergoing rapid change. In summary, this study found that engagement was directly influenced by how satisfied the nurses were with the service that they were able to give and that situations that meant they were not able to provide service at a level they were happy with resulted in frustration and disengagement.

Studies in Australia with police officers and nurses also highlight findings that might apply to librarians. Policing and nursing are considered to be professions that require a high level of emotional labor. Emotional labor refers to the process that employees undergo to control their emotions when dealing with customers and to react in ways that are defined by their employers. Jobs vary a great deal in the amount of emotional labor that they involve, but generally, the higher the level of interaction with the public, the higher the level of emotional labor. Similarly, librarianship requires that everyone who deals with the public reacts in a positive manner, regardless of the situation, resulting in high levels of emotional labor. Jobs requiring emotional labor have been shown to require consistent supervisor support and a buffering of the requirements of the job with a high level of resources in order to create an environment that nurtures employee engagement (Brunetto et al., 2014).

Management literature tends to focus on increasing employee engagement as a means to an end, generally a higher level of productivity that will result in increased profit, and often recommends a piecemeal approach. A more holistic approach, in which a higher level of engagement is the preferred outcome, is the one presented in this book. This approach assumes that there is an array of outcomes of a higher level of employee engagement, both for the individual and for the organization, that go far beyond productivity. Thus, rather than specific changes to increase engagement, this perspective focuses on creating a more positive work climate that includes many ways for employees to be involved, strategies for including employees in management, and a supportive organizational culture, which will nurture employee engagement as well as having other positive outcomes (Jenkins & Delbridge, 2013). As library and information workplaces rarely have a profit motive, this approach is more suitable.

BURNOUT

Burnout has often been described as the opposite of engagement. Where disengagement refers to the reduction of engagement, perhaps to a very low level, burnout goes beyond this absence of engagement into a situation with specific and measurable negative symptoms. This is an expression that is frequently used in a casual way, but for researchers, burnout includes measurable levels of exhaustion, cynicism, and feelings of lack of accomplishment or success, not just as a temporary response to a particular situation but as an ongoing experience as well (Maslach & Leiter, 2008). People who are burned out feel exhausted, constantly overextended, and as if they have no more emotional, mental, or physical resources to commit to their jobs. Their cynicism is demonstrated through a negative or detached response at work and can be described as the feeling that every day is a bad day. Employees who feel this way express the sense that it is a waste of energy to care about their jobs or that nothing they do makes a difference or is noticed or appreciated. As their cynicism grows, it appears that all of their time is spent on tasks that are either mind-numbingly dull or completely overwhelming. Their self-evaluation becomes negative and manifests itself in feelings of incompetence or lack of achievement or productivity. This may occur regardless of others' assessment of their work.

While exhaustion is the most commonly reported symptom of burnout, it is not the only symptom. Exhaustion is a reflection of working too much without a break, being expected to do too many things by too many people, taking on too much responsibility without sufficient support and a lack of supportive relationships. As employees become increasingly exhausted, they tend to distance themselves from their work, and it is this strained relationship with work that distinguishes employee burnout from other forms of exhaustion. In other words, getting more sleep is not the solution. This distance may be seen as employees' attempts to create space between themselves and the source of their exhaustion. As the employees pull away from their work, it increases their feelings of reduced effectiveness or accomplishment.

Burnout is a response to stress but is more significant than a negative response to the stressors of everyday life. It has been shown to lead to a variety of physical outcomes for individuals, including headaches, gastrointestinal problems, muscle tension, increased susceptibility to colds and flu, and problems sleeping (Maslach & Leiter, 2008). Burnout has also been linked with many negative organizational issues, including reduced job satisfaction, reduced commitment, and higher levels of absenteeism. Additionally, burnout has been shown to have a spillover effect, affecting other people both in the workplace and at home.

So what are the causes of burnout? The most commonly identified cause is workload, but it appears that the causes are more complex than too much work and include levels of control and autonomy, perceptions of fairness, the nature of the work community, and the fit between the individual and his or her workplace.

When employees describe problems with workload, they refer to their sense that there is just too much to do, and it has both quantitative and qualitative elements. Eventually, people respond by feeling that they no longer have the capacity to meet goals or deadlines, leading to burnout when there is no period to recover from their work demands. Thus, a particularly stressful event such as a deadline or crisis does not generally lead to burnout as employees recover during less stressful times at work or during nonwork times at home. When too much work starts to be a regular occurrence, however, and not an occasional event, it becomes unsustainable as employees no longer have the opportunity to recover. The conditions are set for burnout to occur.

Employees who experience greater levels of control over their work are less likely to experience burnout. Lack of control is often experienced through role conflict and role ambiguity as well as the feeling that rules and procedures are oppressive and act as a barrier to employees doing their best work. Role conflict occurs when employees feel that they are being asked to do two incompatible things. Academic librarians may experience role conflict with faculty status as it provides the conflicting expectations of being a librarian and being a faculty member (Hosel, 1984). It often occurs when two different systems within the workplace collide, for example, when the financial system expects there to be fewer employees and the service system expects a higher quality of customer service. This results in the common requirement to do more with less. Role conflict can come from different priorities within the same organization, participation in multiple groups, such as serving on more than one committee, or a conflict between personal values and the expectations of the job. This is another situation in which the psychological contract plays a part.

Role ambiguity also plays a part in an employee's perception of the level of autonomy that he or she has. It is described as a lack of clarity about the employee's role within the organization, including what tasks he or she is expected to undertake and what his or her areas of responsibility are. This confusion may be caused by lack of information, lack of clear communication, or the perception of contradictory messages. One source of contradictory messages occurs when a job description is outdated, and an employee is getting new information about his or her responsibility that is not aligned with his or her written expectations.

Unlike many other descriptions of relationships between employees and their work, there is a considerable amount of both research and practitioner literature about librarians and burnout. A quick database search returned more than 500 articles on the subject, dating back about 35 years. Unfortunately, few of them reflect empirical research, and therefore, it is not clear why this is such an area of study. Do librarians experience an unusual level of burnout, or are they particularly susceptible to if for other reasons? It has been proposed that burnout is the result of a career that values always putting the needs of others first. The problem appears to be universal, as there are articles about burnout in librarians from many different countries. They also refer to librarians in many different settings, including schools, public libraries, academic libraries, and special libraries.

Burnout in librarians has been described as a "passion deficit" (Christian, 2015), which clearly links it to employee disengagement. In addition to the causes of burnout identified earlier, work overload and lack of control, there seem to be some issues that are more significantly identified with librarianship. Dealing with unpleasant people, lack of opportunities for advancement, and poor management are also related to other professions, but librarians seem to be more affected by a lack of recognition and a lack of understanding of their professional roles. This occurs on top of an environment of rapid change, reduced funding, and more competition, where librarians feel a need to constantly defend their professional value and their status (Christian, 2015).

A number of articles in the practitioner literature cover how to prevent burnout, but they focus on things that an individual can do to manage their emotional responses rather than on things that management can do to improve the climate of the workplace. Interestingly, there is an opinion piece written for *Library Journal* in 1990 that points to management's responsibility for creating a workplace that does not result in burnout (White, 1990). The author suggests another cause for burnout that is specific to librarians, referring to the moral imperative that librarians must provide excellent service regardless of the level of funding or staffing that is available. He suggests that this leads librarians to accept unrealistic expectations resulting in frustration, anxiety, and, eventually, burnout.

The articles pointing to organizational responsibility tend to provide general descriptions, including ensuring that managers know the symptoms of burnout in order to identify it among staff members and increase employees' knowledge about stress management (Ollendorff, 1990). It seems that stress management and the prevention of burnout are still considered to be an individual's responsibility and not that of the organization.

It is clear that burnout is an important consideration when discussing employee engagement. Individuals who are exhibiting the symptoms of burnout are not able to bring energy and enthusiasm to work. Thus, when considering the potential role of management in creating a work climate that nurtures engagement, it is also important to create a work environment that reduces the stressors that lead to burnout.

ORGANIZATIONAL CHANGE

Since change in library and information environments is frequently cited as a source of stress and negative reactions, it is helpful to review the literature about organizational change and its effect on employees. While there are articles about the need for change in libraries, and pointing to the constant level of change, there is very little empirical research into the impact of change in this environment. The literature from other public service and professional fields, however, can suggest areas of concern.

While organizational change is generally cited as a source of stress, it is not necessarily perceived this way by employees. In some cases, the change is intended to reduce stress by reallocating workloads, by clarifying reporting structures, or by improving role clarity (Smollan, 2016). The impact of the change is also highly dependent on the process for change: a process that includes a high degree of employee participation may actually reduce stress.

A change that is not supported by adequate time or resources, however, will increase stress, particularly if it appears that resources are being taken from key activities. This level of stress is additional to whatever level of stress existed prior to the change as the change process requires greater demands from staff. Stress is increased when there is poor communication about the intent and the process of change, there is an increased level of uncertainty, the change is considered to be unfair, or if the change occurs too quickly or too slowly (Smollan, 2016).

The purpose of organizational change is one of the key factors that determines whether the end result will be an increased level of stress among employees. Unfortunately, many public service changes are interpreted to achieve financial and efficiency goals, without regard for levels of customer service.

The outcomes of increased levels of stress are negative to both the employee and the organization, even if they fall short of the levels needed to induce burnout. These outcomes are serious enough that the World Health Organization has categorized the consequences of stress into physiological, behavioral, emotional, and cognitive, pointing out that they are often linked. Examples of physiological responses to increased stress are headaches and back problems. Behavioral problems include increased irritability and increased aggression; emotional problems include anxiety and depression; and cognitive problems are often described as problems with focus and concentration (Smollan, 2016).

Negative individual responses affect the workplace in many ways. There is the spillover effect and the sense that stress is passed from one person to another. Stressful change experiences have been linked to increased levels of sickness and injury, irrational and unpleasant workplace behavior, increasing levels of negativity, and even cognitive impairment (Smollan, 2016). Reduced ability to complete work responsibilities, absenteeism, and increased levels of accidents affect everyone in the workplace.

Stress during organizational change begins as soon as employees are aware of the impending change, either through rumours or through changes in management behavior. This occurs in spite of the fact that the nature of the change and the process of change may not yet have been determined by management. Stress typically becomes more intense during the change, particularly for those who believe that their positions will be affected. Staff members often become angry or disillusioned if they believe that there is insufficient consultation over the process or intention of the change. Perceptions of lack of management support may be interpreted as lack of caring, lack of awareness of the stress that is being caused, or lack of ability for managers to manage their own stress during the change. The level of stress is often increased by the anxiety of waiting to see how roles will be affected and by heavier workloads resulting from involvement in managing the change while still meeting the expectations of a current position.

A specific frustration during periods of change has to do with timing. Waiting for new job descriptions and new organization charts is often identified as being particularly stressful. While management may see these as a later step in the change process, it is often the thing that employees want to know as soon as possible in order to reduce their sense of being uprooted from their jobs without a specific destination for the future. Even when these changes are implemented, the stress does not necessarily go away. Employees now need to adjust to new expectations, new styles of management from new supervisors, and new relationships with coworkers (Smollan, 2016).

Stress levels following organizational change depend a great deal on the success of the change process and the nature of the outcomes. Employees who are stressed as a result of learning new processes or adapting to new work units generally find that their stress levels reduce as they gain experience and adapt to their new situations. It is important to note that the impact of change on managers is also a consideration. They also experience similar heavier workloads and may also feel guilty about the impact on their staff, particularly in cases where there is a reduction in resources or an expectation of doing more with less. It is necessary for managers to identify and manage indicators of their own stress, as it has a negative impact on the employees whom they supervise (Smollan, 2016).

REFLECTION QUESTIONS

The questions below can be used for personal reflection or to stimulate discussion in staff groups.

1. Individuals experiencing or approaching burnout express feelings of disillusionment, frustration, and lack of accomplishment. For managers, it is important to recognize symptoms of impending burnout in yourself as well as your

employees. Some of the indicators that you may want to consider follow. To what extent do they describe how you feel about your job?

(a) Regularly feeling exhausted by the thought of having to go to work or the thought of what you need to accomplish there.

(b) Regularly feeling that you are not accomplishing what you want to accomplish.

(c) Feeling constantly irritated by coworkers.

(d) Feeling frustrated by management's inability or unwillingness to give you the resources that you need to do a good job.

2. Many writers provide suggestions for how to manage your own stress at work and how to prevent burnout. These include ideas such as health habits for eating, sleep and exercise, taking a break from technology, learning to set boundaries, and adopting creative hobbies. To what extent do you think that employees are responsible for managing their own stress, and to what extent do you think that this is a management responsibility? Do you think management has an additional responsibility to ensure that employees have the skills to manage their own stress by offering stress management workshops, or is this a way of sidestepping the organization's responsibility to provide a safe and healthy workplace?

———

2

Fairness at Work

Workplace climate is the sum of people's perceptions and feelings about their work environment, how it affects their general sense of well-being and their ability to function at work. It is often confused with workplace culture. Climate can be improved and managed by the organization in a straightforward manner, with the result that employees will feel more connected with the organization and its goals and experience reduced levels of stress. Culture is often described as the personality of the organization. It is harder to change, as it is based on history and emphasizes the generally unspoken assumptions about the values of the organization and how things are done. A positive climate is not the same as having more fun at work; rather it is about creating and sustaining an environment in which people feel they can do good work.

Organizational culture evolves over time. Sometimes the change comes about in an evolutionary fashion, and sometimes it is the result of a deliberate management strategy. Managers need to take the lead in changing culture, and it requires a sustained effort on the part of all managers. Changing an organizational culture requires a clear understanding of what needs to be changed and then a strategy that is closely woven throughout all of the organization's activities. Many attempts to change culture fail because old values and behaviors are not addressed, and eventually they return.

Organizational climate refers to the structure that determines how employees experience and interact with the culture. For example, an organizational climate may be goals-based, rules-based, or employee-based. A beneficial workplace climate provides both individual and organizational benefits. It has a positive effect on morale and motivation and provides support and resources that allow people to do their best work. This results in a greater level of job satisfaction with reduced stress reported by employees.

All of this adds up to employees who are able to work toward organizational goals and be committed to the organization.

So what does a good workplace climate mean? A good workplace climate is one in which employees believe that they are able to accomplish things that they consider to be worthwhile and remain involved in their work. It is one in which employees have confidence in the leadership of the organization. In addition, they believe that they receive the support and help from both coworkers and management to do their jobs well, and it is clear to them how they fit into the organization. Conversely, a climate in which an employee is constantly stressed and feels unable to get necessary things done would not be considered a good workplace climate.

The elements of a good workplace climate include a high level of organizational justice as well as a balance between the resources provided and the outcomes expected. This chapter will look at organizational justice as a factor that can be deliberately managed and improved by all levels of management.

ORGANIZATIONAL JUSTICE

Organizational justice refers to people's perceptions of fairness at work. It is important to note that it is completely subjective, and therefore, it is important for managers to understand how their behaviors are perceived by employees. When people believe that they have been treated unfairly, they may respond in ways that have a negative impact on the organization, including reducing their effort and reducing the level of attention paid to their work. People who believe that they are treated fairly have positive reactions that have a beneficial impact on their employer, including intending to stay with the organization, and more focus on assigned responsibilities. In order to understand employees' perceptions of fairness, this chapter will start by reviewing the literature and then discuss how it can be applied in the library and information environment.

Research into organizational justice identifies at least three distinct dimensions: procedural, distributive, and interactional justice. Many researchers have suggested that there is a fourth dimension, informational justice. Each of these will be discussed separately, but they frequently interact.

Organizational justice is important to any consideration of employee engagement because of its link with the psychological contract. In the case of a breach of the psychological contract, the negative impact seems to be reduced by a high level of organizational justice, perhaps because it fulfills at least part of an individual's expectations about how they should be treated.

Procedural Justice

Procedural justice refers to the perception that decision making follows specific rules, including being based on accurate information, being consistent among different people and at different times, reflects current ethical standards, and offers a process for correcting errors. Many researchers believe that for procedural justice to occur, the individuals who are involved in making decisions or affected by the outcome must have input into the process.

Procedural justice shows a strong relationship with work performance, while a lack of procedural justice is correlated with counterproductive work behavior. This is behavior that is not necessarily malicious, but it is always conscious. Employees can demonstrate their feelings by being late for work, theft of small items, gossiping, or providing poor service to customers. Reactions to a lack of procedural justice are generally directed to the organization, which is believed to be the source of the problem.

High levels of perceived procedural justice have been linked with people doing their jobs with energy and commitment and also show a high correlation with work engagement. It has also been shown to reduce the negative impact of psychological contract breach. Procedural justice has so many positive outcomes that one might wonder why all organizations do not strive for high levels of success in this area.

Procedural justice is based on the belief that how a decision is made is as important as the actual decision for those people who are affected by it. It is strongly represented in most union or faculty association contracts, which clearly spell out how decisions regarding working conditions are to be made, including timelines and accountabilities, and remedies if these procedures are not followed. But there are many other procedures in the workplace that must also be considered. Researchers have discovered associations between procedural justice and performance appraisals, recruitment, compensation decisions, participation decisions, bargaining, and strategic decision making, among other things. Clearly, it has a major impact on the workplace.

Most managers have an intuitive understanding of procedural justice and can identify experiences of both good and bad procedural justice that they have experienced, when they are directed to do so by being asked specific questions. This does not necessarily naturally translate into behavior, particularly when they are under stress. Many people are not able to accurately assess how their behavior will be interpreted by others.

Perceptions of procedures that are understood to be fair tend to share the same characteristics. Decisions should be unbiased and should not show any self-interest on the part of the decision maker. Standards should be consistent regardless of who they are being applied to or when they are being applied. Reliable and accurate information should be used as the basis for decision making. It is important that there be a process that allows for an individual to challenge or appeal decisions and that the concerns of everyone involved be reflected in the final decisions. Finally, moral and ethical standards should be incorporated into the decision making. Given that moral and ethical standards are subject and vary among individuals, it is clear that good communication will be an asset to procedural justice.

These characteristics are moderated by other factors. When people do not like the outcome of a decision, they are far more likely to scrutinize the process that was used to make the decision. Timing has also been shown to influence perceptions of procedural fairness. Information received early in a process has been shown to have more impact on perceptions of fairness than information received after a decision has been made. Giving people an opportunity to provide input does not, in itself, guarantee perceptions of fairness.

Input that is requested and appears to be ignored actually has a more negative impact than if no input was requested. If employees come to believe that a manager is just pretending to listen to them but has no intention of considering their input, they are likely to stop participating or, in some circumstances, begin to act in negative ways. This is common even in organizations that believe that they are strongly committed to participative management. In some cases, managers may feel that they are required to ask for employee input even if they have no intention of using it.

Even though it is not possible to reflect everyone's input in a final decision, managers must still find ways to demonstrate that they are listening. This can include being patient and making an effort to understand various viewpoints, particularly those which may be contrary. Verbal acknowledgment of input adds to individuals' beliefs that their opinions are at least being considered, if not implemented. Perceptions of fairness also build over time, and individuals who believe that their manager listens and is fair will be more likely to accept a negative outcome in the future (Barsoux & Manzoni, 1998).

What are the causes of managers behaving in a way that is believed to be unfair, and in particular, not following procedures? Managers may be seeking a more expedient way to get a decision made if they are under pressure to get something done quickly. This is often stated as a reason and in many organizations appears to be the rule rather than the exception. Managers can improve their skills in participative management by checking, rather than assuming, the urgency of decision making. Some managers have a perception about the amount of individual power and discretion that they should have in decision making that is not shared by their employees. They may also be uninformed about the procedures in place for making a particular kind of decision, which suggests that there may be a need for better training for managers.

In order for procedures to be followed, they must be effective, accessible, and usable, and their use must be reinforced. This is as true for managers as it is for any other employees. Reasons for managers not following procedures carefully are often found by examining these characteristics. Procedures that are out of date, incomplete, poorly designed, or not integrated with other policies are ineffective and unlikely to be followed. In order for procedures to be implemented, managers must both know they exist and be able to find them. If they cannot, they may assume they do not exist and find their own approach to decision making, which undermines consistency and standardization, both of which are essential to procedural justice. Procedures need to be usable, meaning easy to understand and providing the necessary information for implementation. Procedures that are outdated, for example, when contact information is not current, create a barrier for even the most well-intentioned manager. Finally, managers, like everyone else, do what gets reinforced. Actions that get noticed get repeated. If there is never any discussion about the process that is used to make decisions, then it is hard to understand the value of those procedures.

Employees take cues, either consciously or unconsciously, from the behavior of their supervisor. Consequently, if it is important in an organization that procedures be followed, managers have to model this behavior. It is not enough to tell staff members how to behave; managers also have to show them. This applies to all levels of management, as each person looks to his or her supervisor for acceptable practices within an organizational context.

Occasionally, managers will not follow procedures because they want to do something that is not allowed, for example, reward a particular employee through allowing additional time off or a more flexible working schedule. They may also ignore procedures because they are reluctant to do something that makes them uncomfortable, such as talk to an employee about inappropriate behavior. The manager may not have considered how this is perceived by other employees or what the impact is on other staff members. It creates a stressful situation for other managers as well, when they do not treat employees in the same way. This applies to sanctions as well as rewards. If an employee comes late, and there is no consequence, other employees may begin to wonder why they make the effort to come on time. This may all point to the need for management training, and, in particular, orientation to the procedures and expectations of a particular workplace.

Distributive Justice

Distributive justice refers to the perception that rewards are allocated in a way that respects principles of equality or equity. Assessment of distributive justice takes into account the amount of reward to be distributed, the process of allocation, and the result of the allocation decision. Managers frequently consider this to be about money, but rewards can also include recognition, opportunities, or privileges. When employees perceive a lack of distributive justice, their negative reactions tend to focus on the individual making the decision.

Distributive justice has been a principle of the labor movement since at least the early 1800s, captured by the slogan of a fair day's pay for a fair day's work. While most would agree with this as not only common sense, but appropriate, there is ongoing difficulty in determining what the meaning of fair might be in a particular situation and whether or not the employer and the employee agree.

One of the challenges of ensuring distributive justice in the workplace is that equity and equality may lead to two different outcomes. Equality suggests that everyone gets the same benefit, while equity may suggest that everyone gets a benefit that is equivalent to the effort that they have contributed. In other words, if you have made a greater contribution, you expect to get a greater reward. Equity, in this case, is often thought of as proportionality. The equity distribution model depends on everyone having an equal opportunity to compete and make a contribution. Many organizations that believe that they distribute rewards, such as increments or opportunities, in an equitable manner overlook the fact that not all staff members have equal opportunity to earn them because of their position or their job description.

A colleague shared this story:

> Our performance appraisal process rewards work over and above a person's regular job with additional pay. This seems really appropriate and there are guidelines that define what kinds of work will be recognized in this way. The problem is that not everyone gets the chance to work on the projects that attract this extra recognition. There seems to be an unspoken agreement that younger colleagues get these opportunities, and consequently they get the extra rewards. This is very depressing as it seems to indicate that the organization prizes youth over experience.

Every time a manager recognizes one employee above another, there is a possibility of being perceived to be unfair, and it is often in the area of distributive justice. Employees may ask themselves why a coworker gets more praise for a job that they both worked on, or why someone else seems to get more opportunities for doing interesting work. Generally, employees feel that they have been treated fairly as long as their rewards are aligned with how much they believe that they contribute. An individual who receives less recognition than another may perceive this is fair if he or she also believes that the other person contributes more than he or she does. Likewise, someone who receives the same reward as another may perceive it is unfair if he or she believes that he or she works harder or contributes more. When a job is filled with an internal candidate, it will be perceived as fair if the candidate is known to be more qualified for the position. When the qualifications are not clear, and there is a perception that the promotion is a result of relationships or favoritism, it is perceived as not being fair. Like many of the other issues in dealing with human resources, it is the perception that results in the outcome, and this is not necessarily the same as reality, as it is perceived by management.

For a manager trying to determine the best way to distribute rewards fairly, the choice of principle (equality, or equity) for guidance can be extremely difficult. There are some guidelines that can help. To begin with, it depends on what the organization is trying to accomplish. Individual achievement and motivation will be supported by an equitable distribution method. The employees who work harder and make greater contributions will be encouraged by their greater reward. If, however, the organization is trying to encourage a team approach, without individual stars, an equal distribution, where all team members receive the same reward, will encourage a sense of group spirit and accomplishment.

Most organizations pay their employees with a blend of the equity and equality models. For example, everyone with the same job gets paid on the same scale and receives the same adjustments for external pressures such as cost of living, which satisfies the need for equality. People who contribute more may be eligible for extra increments, which satisfies the need for equity. This is clearer when dealing with money than it is when dealing with other perceived rewards. How does a manager ensure that everyone has a fair opportunity for promotion or to be part of a new initiative? This is where the other components of justice, such as procedural justice, play a part.

Reward systems need to accomplish a balance of accomplishing two different goals simultaneously. Individuals need to be encouraged to do their best work, and teams need to work together for the accomplishment of organizational goals. This balance can be difficult to achieve as these goals require different distribution patterns for rewards. When there is a high level of difference in wages among a group of employees, they typically report less job satisfaction and also show less collaborative effort (Cropanzano, Bowen, & Gilliland, 2007), which is contrary to good teamwork. This can create tension in library and information settings, particularly in cases where professional staff are paid considerably more than support staff, even though their duties appear to overlap. It is particularly challenging in situations where there are teams that include both professional and support staff.

Paying everyone at the same level, however, is not the solution. The external marketplace has an effect on pay level and retention of employees. If they are underpaid relative to what they can make elsewhere, they may choose to leave. This is particularly true of high-performing employees or those with particularly sought-after skills. It appears that there is no way of paying people that will make everyone happy. Procedural justice, having and using clear procedures for determining pay levels, will make employees, even those who are paid less, feel more comfortable with the way they are paid and less likely to be critical of their employer.

Distributive justice also includes the notion of fair distribution of responsibility. This becomes critical in situations where employees want, or are granted, more input into management decisions. Some employees may perceive that an increased requirement for contribution to planning activities or the implementation of new programs is a stressful addition to their real job, and they may feel exploited by the need to do work that they believe belongs to management. Other employees seek opportunities to provide input and feel that it is an essential part of being a member of the workplace organization (Osawa, 2011). Managers are then left with the dilemma of whether to require participation or encourage and reward it. Each choice has consequences: requiring participation may result in poor quality outcomes and resentful staff, while encouraging participation means that the manager must ensure that everyone has equal opportunity to participate, even if they choose not to.

In many library and information workplaces, committees are established to manage particular services or to develop plans for new services. How is participation on these committees managed in a way that employees perceive to be fair? Does management provide an opportunity for all employees to belong to these committees if they want to, or is it an expectation of all employees? Does participation on some committees, particularly those which are launching new services, provide greater opportunity for reward than participation on other committees? These are questions that are fundamental to thinking about the fair distribution of work in an organization.

Distributive justice is also a consideration when the outcome is not desirable. When the manager is allocating boring tasks, undesirable shifts, or working with a difficult client group, the same considerations of fairness apply. The same principles arise: Should the tasks be distributed equally, that is, with everyone taking their share, or is there another way they should be fairly allocated? Procedural justice can help with this, by providing guidelines for distribution that will be seen to be followed.

Interactional Justice

Employees expect to be treated with dignity and respect in the workplace, and the perception of how they are treated is called interactional justice. It is linked to communication processes and is generally focused on the interaction between an employee and a supervisor, although it may also include interactions with coworkers. Increasingly, reports of incivility in the workplace are being identified as sources of employee dissatisfaction and stress. A recent study of nurses reports that up to 85% had experienced a level of workplace incivility (Warrner, Sommers, Zappa, & Thornlow, 2016).

Managers have a specific role in modeling appropriate interactions with others and expecting them as a norm in the workplace. Interactional justice is characterized by respectful behavior, supported by good communication and interpersonal skills. This involves considering and monitoring the impact of one's behavior on others, not just language but also listening skills and body language. Negative emotions such as anger and frustration must be managed in a way that is appropriate for the workplace.

Interpersonal behavior that can be perceived as a lack of interactional justice is anything that is interpreted as offensive, abusive, intimidating, or insulting. This negative interaction can range from something mild such as lack of support to something that is perceived to be much more threatening. The result of this behavior is that employees feel upset, humiliated, or stressed. In more extreme cases, harassment and bullying are also not only inappropriate but add to the perception of an unfair workplace as well. Library and information environments may be hampered in their identification of bullies because of the general perception that they are safe workplaces. While this may be broadly true, any situation where there are complex personalities combined with issues of status and fairness creates the potential for conflict. Rather than recognizing bullying as an unacceptable behavior, managers and colleagues may tell employees to "toughen up" or to stop being so sensitive (Motin, 2009). This compounds the feelings of unfairness.

A colleague shared this story:

> I was very excited to start a new job as a branch manager at a large library; it was a definite upward move in my career. When I arrived, I couldn't understand why the other branch managers treated me so coolly. It was a series of small things at first—not letting me know if meetings changed locations, and not inviting me for lunch after branch managers' meetings when they all went for lunch together. Eventually I found out that they thought I shouldn't have gotten the job, that one of the other branch managers really wanted it. The bullying got worse, but was still a series of little things—not answering or responding to phone calls or requests, for example. Eventually I went to our boss and asked for help, hoping for some coaching or guidance so I could fit in with the group. He asked me what I had done to elicit this kind of behaviour. I left the job shortly afterwards, feeling not only stressed but unproductive and incapable of doing my job.

Managers may inadvertently contribute to perceptions of interactional unfairness if they are unaware of the effect that their communication style has on others. Two strategies that managers can develop that will improve their level of interactional justice are listening and facilitating. Being a good listener is an essential skill as it helps ensure that you have the right information when you are interacting with an employee. It is particularly useful when emotions are running high and when employees are sharing ideas and feelings. People feel acknowledged on a personal level when their feelings and ideas are heard and confirmed. The basics of good listening include paying close attention to what is being said, allowing others to finish, and repeating what you think you have heard to ensure accuracy. Facilitating a conversation is a skill that keeps the discussion moving forward while recognizing and respecting the input of others. It includes three steps that continue in a cycle until the discussion is complete. To facilitate a conversation, an individual must hear what has been said, integrate it into the topic that is being discussed, and then add more information to move the conversation forward.

A high level of interactional justice, treating people with civility and respect, can help to mitigate problems with distributional justice. This should lead managers to appreciate that even if there are systemic problems within their organization with how rewards and opportunities are distributed, at a personal level, they can improve the situation by managing and improving their interactions with people. They can also practice good conflict management to ensure that staff members are consistently treated appropriately by coworkers.

Informational Justice

Informational justice refers to individuals' perception that they have been given a sufficient level of high-quality information in a timely manner. For example, in the workplace, staff members want information about why things have been done in a particular way or explanations about the distribution of rewards. When people talk about the need for better communication in an organization, they are often referring to their sense that there is a lack of informational justice. Employees need information in order to evaluate decision-making procedures and decisions as well as for interpreting outcomes of decisions. Reactions to decisions such as work assignments are shaped by the quantity and quality of information that is provided about how and why those decisions were made. Perceptions of a high level of informational justice are related to reduced levels of uncertainty and increased levels of employee engagement.

Despite managers being able to explain why news, particularly bad news, needs to be explained fully to employees, many choose to distance themselves from staff when they are delivering news. This often happens at a time when detailed explanations and respectful interactions should play a particularly important role, for example, when explaining a poor performance review or talking about changes that will result in an unexpected outcome for a particular employee. It is difficult to explain why managers have a tendency to do this and consequently make something that is already difficult worse.

One contributing factor is that people are generally reluctant to give bad news and find it very stressful. They may fear the reactions that they believe will follow. The person delivering the news needs to put a great deal more time and effort into providing detailed explanation, being polite no matter what the reaction, and consistently demonstrating respect and concern. It becomes even more difficult for managers when they feel that they are partly responsible for the decision, and this often results in a tendency to distance themselves both by providing less information and by keeping the interaction as impersonal as possible (Patient & Skarlicki, 2010).

Managers often feel some ambivalence about delivering news that will be disappointing to the listener. This is a result of their position in the organization trying to balance two perspectives that may be in conflict, that of the employee and that of senior management. When the news has been delivered, the manager must find a way to listen to the employee's reaction and help to manage the emotion, without getting into a debate about the merits of the decision. In order to soften the blow, many managers are tempted to agree with the employee about the unfairness of the decision, but this leads to further confusion. Sharing their perspectives on the decision is not only unhelpful, but it can also lead to greater negative consequences.

Although supervisors often have relatively little control over the organization's decision-making process, employees typically hold them responsible for how they share information and the amount of information that they share. Employees tend to hold their direct supervisor responsible for the interactional and informational aspects of justice. Within a work group or team, there is often consensus about the level of informational justice, and this shared belief is referred to as the justice climate.

Informational justice has been shown to be particularly important during times of organizational change and has a significant effect on employees' commitment to the change and to the new organizational structure after the change. Since people's concerns about fair treatment at work tend to increase in times of uncertainty, it is essential that they perceive a high level of fairness during organizational changes. If the manager is consistent and sincere in providing details and reasons about changes, employees will experience reduced skepticism and a greater level of security, which allow them to retain their feelings of commitment to the organization (Shin, Seo, Shapiro, & Taylor, 2015).

Sometimes managers do not share information fully because they do not perceive that it is part of their job, particularly when it involves sharing unpleasant information. This is often true in environments where managers are not held accountable for communicating information to staff. They may also feel that they do not know enough about the topic to discuss it freely with staff and fear being asked difficult questions. This situation becomes increasingly complex the more hierarchical the organization is, as managers can only share what they have learned from their managers. In some cases, managers are asked not to share critical elements of information by senior management, in which case they must be clear about their limits and share what they can. If employees do not trust their direct manager, they will believe that he or she is hiding something from them deliberately. It is for this reason that a sense of trust and fairness needs to be developed and maintained over time.

Some managers are information hoarders or believe in sharing information only on a need to know basis. Sometimes they feel the need to hang on to the information because that is the way to protect their power and position. Unfortunately, the opposite is likely to happen as their employees become more uncomfortable. Employees who lack information through formal channels will begin to develop or seek out informal channels to fill their information needs. Unfortunately, these information channels or grapevines are more often sources of speculation and negativity. Information hoarders often believe that they are protecting their staff from things that are too complicated or that will add work to already busy employees. To the employees, however, it appears that their managers do not trust them and that their relationship with their manager resembles a parent-child relationship. This is the antithesis of a transparent organization.

Better communication is often the response when employees are asked for suggestions about how to improve their work environment. Many managers find this frustrating because they do not really understand what their employees want to know or believe that they are already spending enough time and energy communicating. Being more specific about what information employees want, and how they want it delivered, can help to increase perceptions of justice in the workplace. Management sets the tone for workplace communication, and if employees are treated with respect and dignity in communications, they are more likely to show these characteristics in their interactions with coworkers and customers.

Providing wrong information and failing to provide sufficient and correct information are major contributors to problems in the workplace. Information needs to be shared when it is still relevant and in a way that as many staff as possible hear it at the same time. Informational justice means, for example, that everyone at work is clear about how their responsibilities contribute to the overall goals of their work unit and the organization. Research suggests that employees have similar expectations about how they want bad news communicated to them. They want sufficient information about what is going on and how decisions are being made. They want an option to provide their perspective, and they want time to process the information. Finally, they want the option of going back for more information or to confirm their understanding. When these conditions are met, employees perceive a positive justice climate and a high level of informational justice (Conrad, 2014).

Organizational Justice and Libraries

Very little literature specifically discusses organizational justice and libraries. There are studies about gender equity, which speak to the various facets of organizational justice without referring to it specifically. For example, gendered language in policies or gendered images imply a problem with procedural justice, since the procedures themselves appear to not be fair. In the same way, supervisor behavior was cited as supporting perceptions of interpersonal justice and promoting a culture that supports gender equity (Jones & Taylor, 2012).

Articles about performance appraisal processes address factors related to organizational justice. Performance appraisals tend to include all factors of justice: procedural justice in ensuring that appropriate procedures are followed, distributive justice in ensuring that the allocation of any rewards is aligned with performance, interpersonal justice referring to the way in which the supervisor interacts with the employee during the appraisal process, and informational justice reflecting the amount and quality of information that the employee receives before and during the process.

One of the key factors in improving performance appraisal activities focuses on the process itself. An improvement in the process involves providing opportunities for staff members to have input into how the process works; levels of indifference arise if the process is perceived to reflect only management's concerns (Edwards & Williams, 1998). An improved and well-understood process is the first step in increasing the level of procedural justice. If the process also addresses the allocation of rewards, it provides a basis for increasing perceptions of distributive justice at the same time.

A frequently cited problem with performance appraisals is the skill level of the manager actually doing the appraisal. In particular, when they are required to deliver comments that are not completely positive, managers may shrink from clear and complete communication. In some cases, this may be the result of being promoted from a job that did not require this type of interaction; in others, it may be a result of managers not having the necessary skills or not understanding their role in this kind of communication. These reflect organizational responsibilities for training and evaluating all supervisors.

A study of part-time librarians also speaks indirectly to organizational justice issues. Participants in the study reported that they did not feel that they got the same level of respect as full-time librarians, although they might be doing the same work. This could refer to either distributive justice, or to interpersonal justice depending on whether they view respect as a reward or a matter of being treated with dignity, or a combination of both (Wilkinson, 2015). They also reported getting paid less than full-time librarians for doing the same work—an illustration of distributive injustice. Informational justice was also referred to indirectly, as part-time librarians reported not being informed of policy changes.

The issue of faculty status and tenure for academic librarians can also be understood as an organizational justice issue. Distributive justice requires that individuals compare what they get with what someone else gets. Depending on the comparator, an individual may feel that he or she is fairly or unfairly treated. When librarians compare themselves with faculty, they often end up feeling that they do not get the same level of respect as they should for the contribution that they make to the success of students and of the university. Faculty status would result in librarians having the same rights and responsibilities as other members of faculty, including rank, promotion and tenure, compensation, and other benefits such as sabbaticals and research funding. It would also change the way in which performance appraisals are done, focusing on outputs rather than behavior.

Many academic librarians believe that getting tenure would make things more equal and support distributive justice, although they do not frame it in this particular way. Whether the anticipated outcome works, and librarians feel a greater sense of justice when they are treated as academics and are eligible for tenure, has not been explored in depth, and opinions are divided (Herring & Gorman, 2003). While there is some evidence that academic status contributes to feelings of fairness, it also contributes to increased negative issues, such as reduced work/life balance (Galbraith, Fry, & Garrison, 2016) and lack of role clarity, thus contributing to an increased level of stress (Freedman, 2014).

Organizational Justice and Employee Engagement

Perceptions of organizational justice have significant correlations with levels of employee engagement. This provides some useful background for ways in which managers can improve levels of organizational justice, resulting in an improved workplace climate and higher levels of employee engagement.

Procedural justice has a positive effect on employee engagement through creating an environment where employees feel safe identifying with the organization and through that identification are willing to bring their passion and energy to their work. Procedural justice contributes to the sense of stability and reduces levels of anxiety due to unpredictability Put simply, people feel more comfortable identifying with and committing to an organization that they believe is fair (He, Zhu, & Zheng, 2014).

This impact appears to be applicable in many cultures. Further research in India found a positive relationship between all factors of organizational justice and employee engagement. The factors interact in such a way that the perceptions of reward distribution, adherence to fair procedures, and interpersonal treatment all have individual influences on employee engagement (Ghosh, Rai, & Sinha, 2014).

Fairness in an organization increases the level of trust that employees have in their employer. As well as increasing their level of safety, it seems to engender a sense of obligation, in that employees owe something to a good employer and will bring their goodwill and energy to work. This suggests that one of the major responsibilities of management is to ensure a fair workplace. Some of these can be achieved through greater levels of transparency, for example, when procedures have to be changed, an explanation of the reasons for the change increases the level of both informational and procedural justice. Allowing for input into the change from the employees who are affected by it also increases the level of interpersonal justice.

The importance of feeling safe is heightened during periods of organizational change. This feeling of safety is a significant factor in employee engagement and therefore requires consistent management attention. As people understand justice not only through what happens to them but also through what happens to others, management must be aware of employees' perceptions of what is going on around them. Effective communication channels, recognizing and addressing employee concerns and ensuring that everyone is treated with respect, will support a climate of fairness and trust.

Performance appraisals are one of the mechanisms of management that clearly link perceptions of justice with employee engagement. Distributive justice provides employees with the belief that whatever rewards are allocated as a result of the assessment process will be distributed in a way that reflects their contribution to the organization and its goals. Procedural justice reflects employees' feelings that all of their colleagues are being treated in the same way, with the same expectations and measures of performance. When employees feel that the allocation of rewards is fair, they assume that the procedures that arrived at the decision were also fair.

Interpersonal justice is the feeling that employees have about the actual interaction with their supervisor: Were they treated as adults, listened to and addressed in a way that respected their dignity? When employees are comfortable with both the amount of information that they have received and their perception that it is true, they feel that they have a greater sense of control over the process and tend to exhibit higher levels of engagement (Gupta & Kumar, 2013).

A colleague from a multibranch library shared this story:

> In this organization, how well you do on your performance appraisal depends entirely on how good your supervisor is at writing the appraisal reports. It seems that all of the extra increments go to people in a couple of units, because their supervisors are better at writing recommendations that management likes. It doesn't matter how hard you work if you are not in those departments. I don't know if my manager needs better training or what, but I don't see how I am ever going to get anywhere unless I transfer to a unit with a different supervisor. I really don't see any point in working hard where I am.

Although the colleague does not know about organizational justice theory, it is clear that what is being described is a lack of perceived distributive justice. There is no faith that the allocation of rewards is linked to the amount or quality of work, merely that it related to a lack of skill on the part of her manager, something over which employees have no control. Her engagement with her current position is also starting to show a decline as a result of this understanding of the lack of a link between her efforts and her rewards.

REFLECTION QUESTIONS

The questions below can be used for personal reflection or to stimulate discussion in staff groups.

1. Consider a time when you feel that you have been treated unfairly at work. In the context of organizational justice, reflect on which elements of the organizational justice model were involved: Was your perception a result of a poor procedure or one that was not applied appropriately? Was it a result of an imbalance between your work and your recognition, or do you feel you were not treated with respect? Now think about whether more information, or information delivered in a different way, would have changed the way in which you reacted. Based on this, you can reflect on your own behavior as a manager.

2. Many organizations speak of their collaborative or cooperative decision-making process, which may or may not reflect what is actually done. When you think about your own organization, does it have a practice of asking for staff input in an open way that provides opportunities for most staff members? Once the input is gathered, does the organization report back to staff about decisions made as a result of the process? How can you as a manager increase opportunities for staff input and contribute to better sharing of decision results?

3

Increasing Employee Engagement

A high level of employee engagement that results in staff members bringing energy and passion to their work has many positive outcomes, both for the individual and for the organization. Engaged employees are fully at work, focused on the performance of their job, and highly connected to the work of the organization and their coworkers. A previous chapter provided a theoretical understanding of employee engagement; this chapter outlines some specific strategies for increasing engagement, both for yourself and among your employees.

Employees are engaged at work when their needs for recognition, direction, inspiration, and purpose are met. From an organizational perspective, these requirements are part of the mission, climate, and culture of the organization. These needs form part of employees' psychological contract and clearly go beyond the simple exchange of labor for money that was the original foundation of paid work. A 2015 study of North American workers (http://go.achievers.com/rs/136-RHD-395/images/Greatness-report-FINAL.pdf) found that fewer than half of the employees who were surveyed were passionate about their employer's mission or found it inspiring or motivating. This is unsurprising, when only 39% of them reported knowing their organization's mission, and a further 61% reported not knowing their organization's values. This is unlikely to engender a strong emotional tie to the workplace, one of the conditions needed for a high level of employee engagement.

According to a recent Gallup report, employee engagement can help organizations to survive, or even thrive, in poor economic times (http://www.gallup.com/businessjournal/163130/employee-engagement-drives-growth.aspx). While this is not specific to the library and information environment, uncertain funding is frequently identified as a barrier to growth and service implementation. The Gallup report goes on to say that during tough economic times disengaged workers wait to see what happens, while engaged employees try to make a difference. This is often demonstrated through new ideas and willingness to participate in change strategies. Organizations where employees show a high level of engagement show higher levels of customer satisfaction and productivity, with lower levels of absenteeism and quality problems, in addition to higher profits. While profits are not a driver for library and information organizations, the other factors contribute to improved success in providing services.

Rather than looking at a fragmented approach to increase engagement for specific outcomes, this chapter outlines a more holistic approach, in which a higher level of employee engagement overall is the preferred outcome. This broad approach results in a more positive work climate with benefits for employees, management, and the organization as a whole. This improved work climate will include many ways for employees to be involved in both strategic and operational decision making, with high levels of perceived organizational support (Jenkins & Delbridge, 2013). As library and information organizations rarely have a profit motive, this approach adapts management research to a not-for-profit setting. When looking at conditions that support higher levels of employee engagement, it is clear that they also support the other positive staff outcomes previously identified.

Conditions that promote employee engagement include the following:

1. Positive and effective relationships with managers and coworkers (Brunetto, Shacklock, Teo, & Farr-Wharton, 2014) and supervisor support (Saks, 2006)
2. Interesting and worthwhile work (Brunetto et al., 2014) and meaningful work (Rich, Lepine, & Crawford, 2010)
3. Sufficient resources to complete work successfully (Brunetto et al., 2014)
4. Perceived organizational support (Rich et al., 2010; Saks, 2006)
5. Autonomy (Carter & Tourangeau, 2012)
6. Role clarity (Carter & Tourangeau, 2012)
7. Organizational justice (Saks, 2006)

POSITIVE AND EFFECTIVE RELATIONSHIPS WITH MANAGERS AND COWORKERS

One of the factors that helps to define positive and effective relationships between employees and managers is a consistent and open style of communication between them (Menguc, Auh, Fisher, & Haddad, 2013). From this, employees infer that supervisors are interested in them as individuals, beyond their capacity to be productive, and this interest extends to being interested in such things as their relationship with their work and their development and future plans.

A colleague shared this story:

> The circulation staff in my unit came to me to identify that one of the librarians was rude to them, and they felt that she disrespected them. In particular, when she entered the library, she walked straight to her office, with her head down, and ignored everyone. When I spoke to her about this, she was surprised that people thought she was being rude. She had significant family obligations, and was simply trying to ensure that she remembered everything that she had to do that day. I suggested that she take the extra couple of minutes to greet coworkers as she entered the library. Although she doubted that this would make any difference she agreed to try it. She was surprised at the impact that it made, and the staff were happy to discover that she, in fact, knew who they were and did not feel that she was more important than they were.

A successful relationship between an employee and a manager also includes effective and appropriate feedback. Paying attention to perceptions of fairness and demonstrating the principles of organizational justice convey respect, empathy, and caring. Candid, clear, and timely feedback, with a communication style that is tailored to an employee's needs, is a characteristic of a manager's intention to maintain a positive relationship with the employee and leads to a sense of psychological safety (Hansen, Byrne, & Kiersch, 2014). Managers who are relationship-oriented help to create a high level of employee identification with the organization. This, in turn, leads to the employee wanting the organization to succeed and a willingness to contribute extra effort to the accomplishment of organizational goals. Increased identification of an employee with the organization results in a sense of belongingness and loyalty, as individuals internalize the values of the organization. The sense of meaningfulness that develops is one of the characteristics of an engaged employee.

A recent study of American librarians found that the issue most identified with workplace stress was difficulties with management, which ranked considerably higher than budget issues (Wilkins Jordan, 2014). Librarians described this as a lack of support, with policies and guidelines that undermined their performance, lack of clarity and consistency, and uneven application of policy. Managers who are not aware of how they are perceived by staff, or do not recognize the value of complaints by their staff as valuable input, are contributing to staff stress and thus reducing the likelihood of employee engagement. A recent study of bullying in academic environments found that 45% of the respondents identified that managers were the ones who initiated inappropriate behaviors that were interpreted as bullying (McKay, Arnold, Fratzl, & Thomas, 2008).

The issue of bad management, which may result from poorly selected or trained managers, is a difficult one to address. The benefits of improvement, however, make it worthwhile to explore. Change does require that some individuals must recognize that they are causing stress in others, and then the organization needs to ensure that they have support and resources to make the necessary changes. Training and coaching in management skills, people skills, and other associated attitudes require commitment and investment. Managers must be evaluated on these skills and held to high levels of performance. While these skills are being addressed in some library and information programs, they need to be continually honed throughout a manager's career. This issue will be addressed again later in a discussion about the role of expectation setting and performance appraisal in creating a workplace that nurtures employee engagement.

Coworker support has also been shown to have a major impact on levels of employee engagement (Menguc et al., 2013). Employees frequently identify the support that they get from colleagues as providing them with a level of psychological safety. Being able to bounce an idea off a colleague and getting constructive feedback and encouragement are regularly spoken of as helpful in reducing stress (Chiller & Crisp, 2012). Unless you are working in a one-person organization, interactions with those with whom you work closely make up a significant part of your day. Helping behavior from colleagues helps to protect from burnout, replenishes energy, and contributes to the overall success of the unit or organization. An additional benefit is that support from a coworker increases the likelihood that an employee will offer help to another coworker, creating a spiral effect (Halbesleben & Wheeler, 2015). For this reason, helping behavior should be formally encouraged and acknowledged. While many organizations espouse the values of teamwork and helping others, their reward systems undermine this value by focusing on individual accomplishment.

Conflict management skills for supervisors are one of the tools needed to increase coworker support. Interventions that build trust among employees and reduce the level of competition and conflict have positive outcomes for both employees and organizations. Employees experience reduced levels of stress, and organizations benefit from the increased level of productive behavior (Halbesleben & Wheeler, 2015). In order to gain from these skills, it is also essential that the organization makes it clear that conflict management is an expectation of managers, and their performance appraisals will reflect their success in using these skills.

INTERESTING, MEANINGFUL, AND WORTHWHILE WORK

In order for work to be perceived as meaningful, the tasks that an employee is engaged with must provide challenge, variety, the ability to use different skills, personal discretion, and the opportunity to make contributions that are perceived to be important (Saks, 2006). Jobs that include these characteristics, supported by supervisor feedback, have been shown to give employees the opportunity to bring more of themselves into the workplace. This is one of the factors that contributes to engagement, and therefore, meaningful work is one of the ways in which employers can nurture employee engagement (Pavlish & Hunt, 2012).

Meaningful work has been described as one of the most important features of a job, ranking ahead of income, job security, and opportunities for promotion (Michaelson, Pratt, Grant, & Dunn, 2014). Because most adults spend the majority of their waking hours at work, their jobs are an important contribution to their identity and to their sense of belonging. The evaluation of whether work is meaningful depends on the employees' values, what they find important, and how their work aligns with their beliefs.

Some of the ways in which managers can increase the meaning of work include thoughtful job design, involvement of employees in decision making, and removing obstacles that inhibit the ability to focus on their work. Good job design balances organizational needs with ways of providing employees with a sense of personal achievement. This can be accomplished through enlarging the job to include additional challenges, job rotation to support learning new skills, or reducing repetitive tasks.

Having an inspiring vision for the organization linked to shared values helps to create meaningfulness. Many organizations spend a great deal of effort in creating a vision or values statement. Unfortunately, many of them will not take the next step and integrate these statements into their operations. Organizations that include both articulation and practice of their vision and values allow people to feel that they are part of something greater and that they are living up to the potential defined in the vision. Meaningful work occurs in environments where individuals feel that the aims of the organization are linked to larger and more universal goals, where there is a sense of psychological safety and where leaders are seen to model the behavior that is expected of others (Michaelson et al., 2014).

When employees are asked to describe what makes a job meaningful, they include the following characteristics: the ability to complete an entire piece of work, work that promotes the well-being of other people, the ability to use a range of skills, the opportunity to use discretion about how to complete tasks, and feedback about both progress and performance (Michaelson et al., 2014). The level of meaningfulness is enhanced when employees have a direct connection to the people whose lives are affected by their work, which results in a situation in which employees are inclined to work harder and be more effective (Michaelson et al., 2014).

A manager cannot be entirely responsible for creating meaningful work for all employees. In order for the organization to be successful, there are always tasks that have to be completed even if no one wants to do them. The various facets of organizational justice can be employed to ensure that this work is distributed fairly among employees. It is still valuable for managers to consider ways to increase the level of meaning in work, however, given the positive outcomes for both the individual and the organization.

While there is little current research about meaningful work in the library and information environment, much of the management literature can be adapted. A 1992 study of library assistants in academic libraries (Thapisa, 1992) found that the participants were frustrated because their work was not challenging and did not encourage creativity or allow them use the range of skills that they had. This aligns with recent research, suggesting that the need to use skills and be successful at overcoming challenges remains constant.

Studies with nurses reported that the three most important things that created meaningfulness in their work were connections, contributions, and recognition (Pavlish & Hunt, 2012). The relationships with patients and families allowed nurses to connect their effort with the people who were affected by their work. Their contributions to helping patients to improve and the impact that they had on people's lives helped to make their work more meaningful. Being recognized for their skill or their contribution confirmed their career choice as having meaning. These findings translate easily into the library and information environment. Increasing opportunities for staff members to interact with library users is something that may be disappearing as library work becomes more situated in an electronic environment, and there are fewer opportunities to serve users face to face. Ensuring that staff members can see the outcome of their work requires attention as they become more physically separated from clients of the library. Factors that nurses identified as reducing their sense of meaningful work included task-focused environments, stressful relationships with coworkers, and unsupportive management (Pavlish & Hunt, 2012). For librarians, this reinforces the need for environments that focus on meeting user needs rather than task completion, strategies that nurture and reward supportive team environments, and management that understands and addresses the needs of employees. In particular, lack of time and lack of resources are interpreted as lack of management support.

Managers can address the question of meaningfulness at work by encouraging staff members to talk about what they need to feel that their work is meaningful and what changes could be made to increase their sense that their work has value. This may require shifting away from a compliance model of management to one in which employees have some freedom to determine how their jobs are done.

A study of people employed in cultural industries in Brazil confirmed that the factors that affect meaningful work—opportunities for learning and development, the usefulness of the work, quality of working relationships, and autonomy and alignment with larger values—remain valid in a different industry and a different culture (Bendassolli, Borges-Andrade, Alves, & de Lucena Torres, 2015). In particular, aligning professional development with individuals' values and interests allows them to be more successful in their work and contributes to the feeling that the work has value. For this to have the greatest impact, professional development must include both a technical level and a personal one that allows for the development of the employee's potential culture (Bendassolli et al., 2015).

A recent study of Taiwanese librarians demonstrated the importance of task variety in supporting employee engagement (Chang & Wu, 2013). This supports research in other environments, showing that employees who are required to engage in a variety of activities during the work day are more likely to feel challenged by the job and feel that their skills are being used. Monotony at work has been demonstrated to lead to stress, which, if unchecked, may lead to disengagement or burnout (Shantz, Alfes, Truss, & Soane, 2013).

SUFFICIENT RESOURCES TO COMPLETE WORK SUCCESSFULLY

Employees need sufficient resources to allow them to be successful in their work. These resources include not only training, time, and material resources but also a positive work environment. Management is seen as being responsible for providing the resources that are needed, so this is an area where managers can have a significant impact on employee engagement.

Studies with social workers have shown that additional stress is added to their work as a result of a form of economic rationalism, which leads organizations to look for strategies that increase efficiency, often at the cost of effective service (Chiller & Crisp, 2012). The result is the sense that employees are constantly required to do more with fewer resources, a feeling that is often shared by librarians. In the library and information environment, it is difficult to demonstrate the economic value of effective service. This feeling, if it is not addressed, has a negative impact on organizational culture, staff morale, and relationships among staff members.

Good supervision mitigates these issues. One of the roles that a good supervisor plays is to create and implement a process where problems and stresses can be explored and discussed in order to encourage reflection and find new approaches and solutions. The supervisory relationship then becomes an important opportunity for learning. Unfortunately, many people find the kind of supervision that they receive less than ideal and may describe it as unsupportive, bureaucratic, or routine (Chiller & Crisp, 2012). In some cases, this results from managers having a lack of time or skill to fulfill their supervisory role or from lack of direction, support, or feedback from their supervisors.

A colleague shared this story:

> I had a supervisor who wouldn't even pay attention to me during one-on-one meetings. She was always looking at her phone or her computer. I would wait and then say, "Maybe we should meet another time?" but she would say,

"No." Then she would continue to put her attention elsewhere. It was helpful when I learned she behaved this way with everyone, not just me. But it didn't solve the problem. Of course, this led to problems when it turned out that we didn't have the same expectations, so projects took more time to complete. I ended up feeling like I wasn't getting any useful supervision.

The need for effective supervision remains throughout a career. Even the most experienced employees need appropriate resources, including feedback and the opportunity for discussion that comes with a supportive supervisor relationship. Effective supervision is identified as one of the most effective ways of preventing burnout in senior staff (Chiller & Crisp, 2012). Managers often face a significant burden when there is ineffective supervision due to a sense of obligation to meet organizational goals regardless of the lack of resources or impact on personal life.

Particular stressors for managers have been identified. Many choose not to engage in professional development activities such as leadership training because they feel that they do not have time. This lack of time reflects heavy workloads combined with insufficient support. Managers are frequently asked to move to new roles within organizations and manage more people. These stressors are more common among high-performing employees, a factor that is often not recognized by senior management (Nikravan & Frauenheim, 2014).

A 2014 study in the United States (Nikravan & Frauenheim, 2014) found that the "work-more economy" attitudes continued after the actual economic situation eased, with employees reporting that they continued to experience reduced levels of the resources that they needed to do their work. In addition, a significant proportion identified that they needed to do more work at home in order to meet the requirements of their jobs. This quickly becomes an unrealistic expectation, contributing to burnout, as employees lack recovery time between stressful work events. An environment where there is a shortage of resources creates competition among employees, which counteracts efforts toward collaboration.

Increasing the expectation of collaboration in the workplace, without reducing the level of any other commitments, has also been identified as creating more stress due to overwork. More complex reporting structures and the time required for collaboration often result in increased time commitments in order to meet goals, and this time is generally not accounted for when allocating responsibilities (Nikravan & Frauenheim, 2014). This has been confirmed in library and information environments; a 2014 study of American librarians found that "lack of time" was one of the top five issues causing stress (Wilkins Jordan, 2014).

Compounding the issues raised by economic tensions is the stress caused by reduced levels of staffing, which is often the outcome of financial constraints. While layoffs might not be implemented, failing to fill positions, delaying recruitment, and a reduction in part-time staff all have negative impacts on employees if workload is not adjusted. Staff members can end up feeling underappreciated, anxious, and frustrated when they perceive that as people leave, more work is expected of them. A study of an American public library reported an increase in tensions among staff as a result of decreases in staff, including more resistance to change, fewer innovations, and more detached employees (Wilkins Jordan, 2014), all factors that are contradictory to employee engagement. The author goes on to say that "these responses to diminishing resources are shared by librarians across the country as they are constantly exhorted to do more with less" (Wilkins Jordan, 2014).

Workplace resources also include appropriate places to work, with sufficient tools. A study of workplace facilities in public libraries identified many ways in which they contributed to staff stress. Repetitive work done at computers, sitting on one place for a long time, and moving heavy items around the library all contribute to neck and back problems and carpal tunnel syndrome (Wilkins Jordan, 2014). Added to this, librarians report depressing surroundings that are shabby or dirty and home to bugs and rodents. These and other and poor building conditions all contribute to burnout, which may be considered to be the antithesis of employee engagement.

A colleague shared this story:

> After I found out that my employer offered an ergonomic review of workstations, I requested a review of my desk. I waited nine months for the review to take place and the needed equipment to be bought and installed. In the meantime, my doctor diagnosed me with repetitive strain from computer work and said I needed physical therapy. Although my employer offered this kind of ergonomic help, I felt that the attitude was that I should go elsewhere if I wasn't happy with the equipment provided.

Another workplace resource is information. Employees need enough information to do their jobs well, and lack of information and unclear expectations about responsibilities result in role ambiguity. This is significantly more important in positions that cross organizational boundaries, such as working in different units of the library, and in organizations that experience frequent changes of technology or organizational structure (Shupe, Wambaugh, & Bramble, 2015). The roles of library staff are constantly evolving as a result of both changes in the information environment and changes in user behavior. These tend to result in role expansion, requiring an increasing level of skill as well as an increased workload.

While there is a considerable amount of attention to stress and burnout in the library and information literature, most of it focuses on what individuals can do to improve their situation: exercise more, sleep more, and find a better balance between work and home (Wilkins Jordan, 2014). There is considerably less attention paid to the responsibility of management to make organization-wide changes that will address this issue. A study of academic librarians that identified the stresses caused by technological change and changes in user expectations called for library management to explicitly address these sources of stress and focus on reducing role confusion (Shupe et al., 2015) and improving the work environment. A clearly defined process that allows library staff members to discuss and clarify expectations with their supervisors, express their frustrations, and ask for the necessary resources to meet goals increases perceptions of fairness and leads to more sense making in the face of changing requirements. This, of course, comes with the reminder that the supervisor must listen respectfully and demonstrate an intention to work toward a solution.

PERCEIVED ORGANIZATIONAL SUPPORT

Perceived organizational support is the extent to which employees believe that their employer cares about their well-being and values their contributions in the workplace. It is one of the ways in which employment fills an individual's social and emotional needs. Studies demonstrate that a high level of organizational support contributes to employee engagement regardless of the age of the employee (Kralj & Solnet, 2011). The perception of organizational support determines the extent to which employees believe that the organization will take care of them and the likelihood that the organization will reward any extra effort that they make. This assessment becomes more favorable when employees have positive experiences at work and believe that these experiences are a result of discretionary decisions made by the employer, as opposed to those that the employer is legally required to make. Employees tend to exchange extra effort and dedication in exchange for emotional benefits, including support for their self-esteem, approval, and a sense that their employer cares about their well-being (Kralj & Solnet, 2011).

Perceived organizational support is related to a perception of psychological safety, which is the sense that employees can show their true selves at work without negative consequences. Environments that include high levels of supportiveness and openness allow employees to try new things, without fear that there will be negative repercussions for failure. Perceived organizational support includes support from coworkers as well as from management. When employees perceive a high level of organizational support, they believe that their organization cares about them and their well-being. This creates a sense of obligation to the employer resulting in employees paying more attention to organizational goals and putting more effort into fulfilling their work expectations as a way of contributing to these goals (Saks, 2006). Since most employees are not in a position to determine how the organization feels about them, their supervisor's orientation is often taken as an indicator of perceived organizational support. This placed additional responsibility on the supervisor as a representative of the organization.

Perceived organizational support also increases employees' sense of self-efficacy, which is their assessment of their ability to complete tasks successfully. This is a result of positive messages and feedback that employees receive as part of evaluation processes. Increasing levels of self-efficacy, in turn, lead to a higher level of absorption in tasks and an increase in the levels of energy and effort that are applied to them (Caesens & Stinglhamber, 2014). This energy and effort is a component of employee engagement.

Perceived organizational support has many benefits for the individual employee as well as for the organization. Employees who perceive a high level of organizational support experience more positive moods and decreased levels of stress. They are more committed to their work and being more conscientious tend to be more innovative (Mitchell, Gagné, Beaudry, & Dyer, 2012).

Some of the ways in which employees' perceptions of organizational support can be enhanced include programs that focus on determining and addressing employees' needs and concerns and those that demonstrate caring and support, such as flexible work arrangements (Saks, 2006). Any program that makes employees feel that their employer cares about them results in a stronger relationship between the employee and the employer. Decisions and actions that lead the employees to believe that their employer trusts them and allows them to feel more autonomous as well as provides the resources that are necessary to meet expectations result in increased feelings of competence. Access to training opportunities and the chance to participate in decision making are also components of perceived organizational support.

A summary of ways in which organizations can increase the level of perceived organizational support for all employees is as follows:

1. Programs that support employee well-being
2. Consideration of individual's opinions and input
3. Acknowledgment of good work and effort
4. Demonstrate knowledge of and pride in individual's accomplishment
5. Consideration of individual goals and values when setting expectations
6. Demonstrate willingness to provide the resources that employees need to be successful

Employees who believe that they are treated well by their organization treat customers better (Shanock & Eisenberger, 2006), an important consideration in library and information environments. Employees with higher levels of perceived organizational support are rated by customers as being more attentive, more courteous, and more concerned about the customer's needs (Shanock & Eisenberger, 2006). In library and information environments, the quality of customer service is an important consideration, as it represents the value added that distinguishes the service from competitors.

In order to behave in ways that will increase employees' perceptions of organizational support, supervisors must feel that they also have support from the organization. Managers, just like other employees, need to feel valued. When they perceive that they are supported, they are more likely to help other employees, provide orientation and coaching to new employees, and generally provide assistance to others to help them meet their expectations. When supervisors report a high level of perceived organizational support, their subordinates report that they are more helpful, more respectful, and more supportive of skill development (Shanock & Eisenberger, 2006). The importance of this trickle-down effect should not be underestimated, as employees typically use the level of support that they get from a direct supervisor as a measure of the overall support that they get from their employer.

While no one likes to think that it could happen in their workplace, there are many examples of abusive supervision, in which supervisors humiliate, ridicule, or in some other way exhibit demeaning behavior to their employees, either verbally or nonverbally. Typically, employees hold the organization responsible for this bad supervisor, because they believe that the employer is both morally and legally responsible for the behavior of its supervisors (Shoss, Eisenberger, Restubog, & Zagenczyck, 2013). The end result of abusive supervision is the belief that the organization does not care for its employees, interpreted as a reduced level of perceived organizational support. To combat abusive supervision, organizations must both articulate a culture of supportive supervision and enact it by evaluating supervisors on their treatment of employees. Employees will look to senior managers to see that this culture is actually the way in which the organization operates. Fair treatment of supervisors will model expected styles of interaction.

While there are no studies that link positive organizational support with the library and information environment directly, research in other areas is relevant. A 2015 review found that there was a strong link between perceived organizational support and employee engagement in both governmental and educational settings (Ahmed, Nawaz, Ali, & Islam, 2015). A study that looked for conditions to increase employees' motivation to use new information technology found that perceived organizational support resulted in improvement in both employees' attitudes and behavior around the use of new of the new technology (Mitchell et al., 2012).

AUTONOMY

In the workplace, autonomy refers to the amount of control that an employee has over determining how and when work gets completed. A high level of autonomy means that employees are able to work with little direct supervision and with considerable freedom in making work-related decisions (Patillo, Moran, & Morgan, 2009). It does not imply complete discretion over work; managers still have the responsibility to set goals and ensure that work contributes to the achievement of the organization's direction. In most workplaces, expectations that contribute to organizational goals have to be assigned; so how can you create a sense of autonomy? The primary step is ensuring that employees know why a task is necessary. Allowing employees to have control over how an expectation is to be achieved allows them to tailor the work to take advantage of their skills and preferences and provide an increased sense of control. Even if there is not completely free choice, providing opportunities for input increases the sense of autonomy. The more employees are encouraged to exercise control over their own work, the more engaged they will be.

A colleague shared this story with me:

> I had a supervisor who went too far. It was more than autonomy, it was indifference to what we were doing. He completely left us alone to do what we thought needed to be done. While each of us know how to do our jobs, we completely lost the sense that we were working together for a common purpose, and we all started to withdraw from our work. It was hard to come to work some days. This was in complete contrast to his predecessor, who outlined goals and directions and then left us discretion over how we actually accomplished things. That supervisor was there when we needed help or feedback, but didn't micromanage. Coming to work every day was a treat.

Individuals vary in their need for autonomy at work, but in general, higher levels of autonomy have been found to have both individual and organizational benefits. Autonomy is particularly important for skilled professional workers who expect greater freedom in exercising professional judgment as well as more control over their working situation, including schedules, location, and pace (Patillo et al., 2009). Several studies demonstrate that the level of autonomy is one of the work characteristics that has a significant impact on how an individual feels about his or her employer (Chang & Wu, 2013).

Researchers define three components of autonomy: content, terms of work, and criteria. Content autonomy refers to the extent to which individuals have control over their work and the methods used to accomplish it. It includes a level of freedom designing and completing substantive amounts of the work. Autonomy in terms of work refers to the level of freedom an individual has in determining both the schedule and location of his or her work. Criteria autonomy refers to the level of independence an individual has in determining the criteria upon which his or her work is evaluated (Patillo et al., 2009).

The amount of autonomy that employees experience is often related to their manager's ability to delegate. There are a number of reasons that managers struggle with delegating to employees, related to their perception of the skill of the employee, the time required for delegation, and the appropriate level of work to delegate. Ultimately, it is a skill that can and must be learned for a manager to be effective and must be part of the expectations and assessment of management positions. Delegation is critical when dealing with professional employees to meet their expectations of autonomy, which are generally higher than those of other employees.

As workload demands increase in many workplaces as a result of economic pressures, managers must seek ways to increase the level of resources available for employees. Autonomy is identified as one of the resources that help individuals to cope well with increasing levels of expectations (Van Yperen, Wörtler, & De Jonge, 2016). Technology allows for a higher level of autonomy by creating opportunities for individuals to work in different locations and on different schedules, either as a result of personal preference or to schedule around other commitments. Blended working refers to time- and location-independent working using technology, in which the individual makes decisions about how work is to be completed. It increases autonomy, which allows individuals the opportunity to effectively manage higher workplace demands.

Several studies show that more flexible working arrangements, particularly those enabling employees to work away from the office, have a positive impact on individuals through improving work-life balance, job satisfaction, and job performance (Van Yperen et al., 2016). The downside of working away from the office includes a sense of being disconnected from colleagues and a lack of structure around work. Because people vary in their need for autonomy, for being connected, and for structure, it is important to distinguish between creating opportunities for people to work in different locations if they want to and forcing them to work at home because their workload is unmanageable during a regular working day.

Since older employees generally have a higher need for autonomy and a lesser need for externally imposed structure, greater levels of autonomy may be a good way to keep them engaged and productive (Van Yperen et al., 2016). A recent study of university librarians in Taiwan found that more experienced librarians reported a higher level of autonomy than those with less experience and confirmed the role of autonomy in increasing both job satisfaction and job performance (Yu-Ping, 2012).

A study of American librarians found that academic librarians reported a higher level of autonomy in their terms of work than did public librarians. Since libraries are strongly influenced by the culture of their context, academic libraries tend to take on some of the characteristics of the academic environment. Academic librarians reported more fluid schedules as well as more responsibilities outside of regular business hours due to committee responsibilities and the need to do research. The authors noted, however, that there was no difference in academic and public librarians' reports of their level of autonomy regarding the content of their work (Patillo et al., 2009).

Regardless of the setting, librarians with information technology roles report a higher level of content autonomy than other librarians. They indicate a significant level of freedom in determining both what work is to be done and how it is to be done, not in terms of their working conditions. The size of the library was not related to the level of autonomy reported by any research participants (Patillo et al., 2009), suggesting that autonomy is a function of management style.

Criteria autonomy is the least directly discussed dimension of autonomy. It is, however, frequently referred to, although not by name, in discussions of performance appraisal processes. When undertaking performance appraisals for librarians, a process that allows participation in definition of performance goals is identified as a hallmark of good practice (McKay, 2015) and a means of reducing anxiety. Librarians may be particularly prone to anxiety during the performance evaluation process as much of their best professional work is difficult to assess without reducing it to a series of disconnected tasks. Giving librarians the opportunity to help define the criteria on which their work will be appraised allows them to clearly define both qualitative and quantitative aspects of their work.

All components of autonomy have been shown to have a significant impact on librarians' perceptions of their work environment (Chang & Wu, 2013). Procedures and controls that are perceived as being overly elaborate and unnecessary undermine a sense of autonomy by communicating to employees that they are not trusted. Autonomy increases librarians' sense of identification with their library (Chang & Wu, 2013), supporting a climate that nurtures employee engagement.

One of the organizational factors that is significant when looking at autonomy is the direct supervisor's autonomy-supportive behaviors. Supervisors who support autonomy provide a meaningful rationale for the work that has to be done, emphasize elements of choice rather than control, and acknowledge the feelings and perspectives of employees (Gillet, Colombat, Michinov, Pronost, & Fouquereau, 2013). In this way, they foster feelings of well-being and enhance performance. Supervisor support for autonomy, then, has a significant impact on the assessment of organizational support, giving employees a level of psychological safety and contributing to employee engagement. Becoming an autonomy-supportive supervisor is a skill that can be learned (Gillet et al., 2013).

ROLE CLARITY

It may seem obvious that the success of an organization depends on all employees knowing what they are supposed to be doing so that they can focus on doing it well. This clarity is often taken for granted by supervisors.

In order for both the organization and the employees to be successful, everyone needs to understand their role and the organization's expectations. Additionally, employees need to understand the role of their managers and supervisors, just as their supervisor needs to understand their role. This leads to everyone being clear what it expected of themselves and others and allows efforts to be integrated and focused on the organization's goals. Role clarity has three components: understanding the expectations about outcomes of a job and how it is to be assessed, understanding the ways in which the job is to be done and the level of autonomy, and knowing the consequences for performance that is either ineffective or effective.

A high level of role clarity reduces uncertainty and stress and contributes to a sense of empowerment. It also contributes to high quality relationships between employees and managers (De Villiers & Stander, 2011) and has a significant impact on the level of employee engagement. It is more complicated than simply providing employees with a job description as role clarity is perceived by employees as resulting from their interactions with their supervisors and related to their supervisor's ability to communicate clearly about what is expected.

Role clarity is also related to autonomy as it sets the boundaries that allow employees to understand the amount of choice that they have in how to do their jobs and also the implications of different choices and actions. It gives employees the most effective amount of influence in how a job is done, while still aligning their work with organizational plans and directions.

Role clarity contributes to psychological empowerment by allowing employees to act with more choice resulting in more confidence as they perform their work. This sense of empowerment has results in higher levels of effectiveness, efficiency, and productivity due to lower levels of uncertainty (De Villiers & Stander, 2011). All of these factors contribute to a greater sense of engagement as employees are better able to contribute their energy and enthusiasm to their work and become more deeply involved with it.

The opposite of role clarity is role ambiguity, which occurs when employees are unclear about their particular jobs and the expectations that are connected with them. This can be focused on a particular project or assignment or may occur overall. One of the contributing factors to role ambiguity is organizational change. As organizations adapt to new environments and economic and political pressures, new positions emerge, and employees are expected to adapt to frequently changing tasks and new or expanded roles. This requires appreciable ongoing adjustment. Role ambiguity may be accompanied by role conflict, which arises when an employee is expected to fulfill conflicting or opposing expectations. This creates a stressful situation in which employees feel that they are not capable of meeting all of the expectations at the same time (Schmidt, Roesler, Kusserow, & Rau, 2014). Both role ambiguity and role conflict have been shown to contribute to depression in employees and to reduce employee engagement.

Some organizational factors contribute to both role ambiguity and role conflict. In an organization where there are a significant number of employees reporting to one supervisor, there may be fewer opportunities for personal interaction, resulting in less information being shared or fewer opportunities to clarify issues that are not clear. Interdependent teams and matrix management models increase the probability of role ambiguity and role conflict as there may be more than one supervisor resulting in different expectations or different interpretations of the same expectation.

It seems logical that employees who are feeling role conflict and role ambiguity need to seek information from their supervisor. There are a variety of reasons why they may be uncomfortable doing this. Employees may feel reluctant to admit to their supervisor that they are unsure of what they are doing for fear that it will be reflected negatively in their performance appraisal. They may fear that it will be interpreted as a sign that they are incompetent or unable to think for themselves. In the past, they may have had negative experiences when asking for feedback or found that the supervisor was unwilling or unable to provide more information. If there is anxiety around requesting information from supervisors, employees often seek it from coworkers, which is only successful if coworkers have accurate information to contribute (Srikanth & Jomon, 2013). One of the strategies that organizations can use when dealing with organizational change and its impact on role ambiguity is to consider ways to increase feedback-seeking behavior among employees.

What can an organization do to promote role clarity? As work environments appear to be more unstable than in the past, it is increasingly important to be clear about roles as well as tasks, responsibilities, and expectations. One of the indicators of this increasing instability is that employees may have several supervisors during their time with the organization. This makes it challenging to develop meaningful relationships between managers and employees. Organizations can simplify these transitions by planning ahead for organizational changes and retirements and ensuring that relationship management becomes one of the criteria for a successful change.

Management training needs to include the skills required to communicate these issues clearly with employees and to recognize and address issues of ambiguity or conflict. Supervisors need to understand and work with the impact of inconsistent or changing expectations. As role ambiguity has been shown to be a major contributor to poor performance, supervisors should be encouraged to explore issues of role clarity when they are addressing performance-related issues. Additionally, supervisors may need assistance in interpreting requests for feedback from employees and learning to interpret them not as challenges to authority but as valid requests for information that will contribute to success.

Increasing managers' skills in giving feedback helps to support role clarity. For feedback to be useful, it needs to provide information that is helpful to the employee. Feedback has two elements that are not always clearly understood or practiced: reinforcing positive or expected behavior and correcting or modifying undesired behavior. Managers exhibit a great deal of individual differences in the extent to which they incorporate both factors of feedback: some are very sparing with reinforcing good behavior and focus their efforts on modifying undesirable behavior, while others are generous with praise but uncomfortable with correction. In either case, they are not providing enough information for optimal role clarity.

Issues of role clarity, conflict, and ambiguity have been extensively studied in the library and information context. As early as 1980, Stead and Scammell identified areas that contributed to role conflict among librarians, including having to do things that they believed should have been done differently, having to break rules in order to carry out work, and trying to deal with incompatible requests. They also considered uncertainty as one of the factors that contributes to role ambiguity and identified two examples: the level of autonomy and lack of clarity about how their work interacted with the work of others. Their findings suggest that role ambiguity is directly related to employee satisfaction with their supervisor, while role conflict affects satisfaction with coworkers, pay, and opportunities for promotion. One of the factors that distinguished librarians from other professional groups was the low level of discretionary power that they had relative to their professional education when compared with engineers, teachers, and scientists. The authors summarize their article with a call for library administrators to be clear about departmental and organizational objectives and how employees are expected to contribute to these objectives (Stead & Scammell, 1980).

This call for clarity has not resulted in the necessary change. Recent studies of librarians show that they still experience stress as they are not able to clearly determine their job-related duties, and are unclear about how to deal with changes in technology. They frequently report conflict between how the way in which they expected work to be done and how it was actually being done (Shupe et al., 2015). Levels of role ambiguity were shown to be comparable with a sample of nursing executives and higher than that experienced by samples of business people and teachers. The role stress experienced by librarians is similar to other employees who regularly use information technology or whose industry is affected by rapidly changing technology.

Shupe et al. (2015) also conclude their article by recommending that library management look clearly at job-related responsibilities, monitor them for change, and explicitly communicate changes in expectations and responsibilities. They add that there is a need for job-related training and professional development to equip staff members to deal with the changes inherent in their work.

ORGANIZATIONAL JUSTICE

Managers who demonstrate a sense of fairness contribute to employees having a sense of meaning in their employment, which helps to support employee engagement. Research shows that managers are aware of the importance of fairness and try to be fair or at least try to appear to be fair. What is important in employee engagement, however, is whether employees perceive managers to be fair. This perception goes beyond any one event and must be understood as a general perception of a manager as being fair or unfair. These perceptions evolve over time, so a manager needs to strive for a consistently fair approach in the workplace.

Managers' self-perceptions of fairness vary, although most have been shown to rate themselves highly. Individual managers may recognize that they are more or less fair in different situations or with different people, understanding that they do not treat everyone in the same way. Some managers consider being fair to be more important than do others, depending on whether it is a quality that they value in themselves. For example, managers who are evaluated on outcomes such as cutting costs or implementing change may perceive being fair to employees as less important than using strategies that will result in achieving those outcomes. Conversely, an organization that rewards a collegial work environment will encourage managers to develop skills, like demonstrating fairness, that encourage people to work together.

Employees evaluate the manager's fairness through the sum of many interactions, including observation or participation in activities with their manager such as performance appraisals, allocation of work tasks, and recognition or appreciation of success. In each event involving the manager and the employee, interactional justice will be considered. Therefore, consistency in treating employees with respect, offering explanations for decisions, and showing a level of awareness of the employee's reaction is necessary to demonstrate interactional justice. For example, when employees ask for help from a manager, they are giving the manager an opportunity to demonstrate respect and attention. The style of the interaction and how the manager responds will have a significant impact on employees' overall assessment of manager fairness (Cooper & Scandura, 2015).

Distributive justice is evaluated by employees in situations where there is a decision to allocate rewards, including praise, tasks, and resources. Procedural justice is evaluated in situations where there is a decision made, and it is necessary to demonstrate that it has been made in an appropriate fashion. Employees make these judgments based not only on their own experience with the manager but also through observation of the manager's interactions with coworkers. When employees believe that their manager is fair, they are often not conscious of having made a judgment. This results in comfortable relationship and leaves the employee's attention to the work at hand (Cooper & Scandura, 2015). Although individuals vary in their tolerance for inequity, as a general rule, a climate of fairness results in an optimal workplace environment.

The reason that organizational justice is treated in such detail in this book is because of its significant role in influencing employee engagement. Situations that are both predictable and consistent help to create a safe environment where employees are comfortable bringing all of their energies and passions to work. Organizational justice is the major indicator of both predictability and consistency at work (Saks, 2006). As well as psychological safety, organizational justice creates obligations for employees: if the organization is fair with them, they feel a responsibility to be fair with the organization by bringing their best efforts to work.

Some suggestions for increasing the level of fairness in your workplace are listed next:

1. Use policies and guidelines for making decisions.
2. Listen carefully and make sure that you have facts and understand the circumstances when making a decision.
3. Explain how the decision was made, including the procedures and the criteria that were used.
4. Take sufficient time to answer employee questions about the decision, particularly for people who will be affected negatively by it.
5. Develop and implement a process of open communication to address issues that are causing stress. For maximum impact, include staff, managers, and members of the community that is served (Wilkins Jordan, 2014).
6. Develop and implement a plan to address conflict and bullying, and ensure that supervisors understand their role in managing this behavior.

CONCLUSION

Changing levels of employee engagement within a particular organization is a long-term and ongoing process, built up over many small interactions continued over time. It is not a quick fix and depends on the ability to consistently treat employees in a way that both creates a safe environment for them to be fully engaged and builds up a sense of reciprocal obligations that encourages employees to devote energy to the achievement of organizational goals. Developing a climate that fosters employee engagement needs to be treated as a broad organizational strategy that involves everyone in the organization and requires input from everyone involved.

REFLECTION QUESTIONS

The questions below can be used for personal reflection or to stimulate discussion in staff groups.

1. When you think about the mission and values of your library, does it engage you and define the kind of organization that you want to work for? Many organizations spend a lot of time drafting these statements but much less time in ensuring that they set the standard for how members of the organization behave. Is your organization consistent in integrating its values into expectations and evaluations, and if not, is there a way that you can increase the level of integration?

2. Very few people are comfortable in managing conflict. When you think about your own career, can you identify conflicts that were managed in a way that seemed fair, leading to a positive or at least neutral outcome? Conversely, can you identify conflicts that were not managed well and created stress and tension? When you review your own skills as a manager, assess what skills you need to develop in order to feel competent at conflict management.

4

Increasing Motivation, Organizational Citizenship Behavior, Commitment, and Perceptions of Well-Being

The interactions between an employee and a job may be described in many ways. Employee engagement is one, but there are others that are of interest to an employer, such as motivation, organizational citizenship behavior, and commitment. Although they are all related to employee engagement, this chapter looks at each of them separately and explains why they are important for both employees and organizations, and how managers can create an environment where they flourish.

MOTIVATION: WHAT IT IS

Motivation at work is simply being eager, or at least willing, to do what needs to be done. It is a result of the interaction between individual traits and organizational circumstances. While managers cannot change individual traits, skill in recognizing differences among individual employees supports different choices in how they are treated (Barrick, Mount, & Li, 2013), allowing managers to create motivating situations. Two aspects of motivation have a significant impact on employee behavior: purposefulness and meaningfulness. Purposefulness refers to an understanding of the outcome that individuals are trying to achieve. Meaningfulness refers to the significance or importance that individuals derive from their work. It appears that, for most people, a combination of these helps to explain their motivation at work (Barrick et al., 2013) as it describes a personal agenda that combines thought and emotion. Of course, each individual has a different mix of these two factors.

The goals in the workplace that motivate people generally have four components, with each having a different level of importance for each individual. Communication goals refer to an individual's need for being connected to others, having friendly relationships, and an opportunity for altruism. Status goals are related to an individual's need for power, prestige, and esteem. Autonomy goals are related to personal growth, and achievement goals are related to competence, prestige, and variety. These four components provide intrinsic motivation that defines the purposefulness and meaningfulness of work (Barrick et al., 2013). The different levels of importance of each component reflect not only an individual's personality but also his or her values and interests. Because of the impact of personality, which is generally stable over time, the goals that are important to people are typically consistent throughout adulthood and can been seen across different work situations.

A particular type of motivation, public service motivation, is defined as a predisposition to serve the community and public interest (Chen, Hsieh, & Chen, 2014). It is a significant factor in the choice of public service employment rather than business employment and results from an orientation toward helping others and serving the interests of the community. Public sector employees, when compared with private sector employees, tend to have a significant interest in serving the common good (Prebble, 2016). This motivation should be of interest in the library and information services environment, as it is aligned with the goals of many information services. It suggests that the desire for meaningful jobs that meet personal needs and align with values may be higher in public service environments.

Why Motivation Is Good for Employees

The conditions in the workplace that support motivation also support an increased sense of well-being, which is simply the sense that an individual has of being comfortable, healthy, and happy. It is linked to having work that matches skills and preferences, with a desirable amount of autonomy. A level of variety, supervisor support, and sufficient opportunities for interactions with coworkers or clients that is aligned with personal preferences supports this feeling of well-being (Biggio & Cortese, 2013). A sense of well-being at work has two components. The first is the sense that the work that you are doing is appreciated as being of value; the second is a positive working climate with good relationships.

Motivated employees view their workplaces as being fairer than do their less motivated colleagues. This positive emotion helps to prevent burnout, and motivated employees also tend to be both physically and psychologically healthier. They report a higher level of contentment with their lives in general and demonstrate better coping skills when things go wrong.

Being motivated at work, leading to a general sense of well-being, has a positive impact on individuals outside of work as work and home lives are interrelated and have a reciprocal effect on each other. The emotions from work will spill over to home and vice versa, so workplace efforts to support motivation have a benefit for employees' home lives. Motivation and well-being are associated with better health and a general sense of energy and enthusiasm about life (Danna & Griffin, 1999).

Why Motivation Is Good for Organizations

Both practitioners and researchers support the idea that having motivated employees is good for an organization. The cumulative motivation of the entire workforce supports the work that is needed for the organization to meet its goals.

Organizations get specific benefits from motivated employees. They experience a higher level of commitment, meaning that they are less likely to leave or to look for another job. They engage in more discretionary prosocial behavior that benefits others, such as organizational citizenship behavior that supports coworkers and contributes to a socially rewarding workplace. Motivated employees are more emotionally involved with the organization, which includes a stronger identification with the organization's values and goals, and therefore tend to be more persistent in their work when conditions are difficult (Battistelli, Galletta, Portoghese, & Vandenberghe, 2013).

Motivated employees perform better. Along with the impact of their individual work, there is a spillover effect on their coworkers. When one person is not motivated to work hard, other employees may feel the need to work harder to make up for it, leading to feelings of injustice, particularly if their extra efforts are not recognized. Poorly performing employees who lack motivation also use up a considerable amount of a supervisor's time, limiting the amount that they can spend investing in encouraging and supporting highly performing employees.

One employee who lacks motivation can have a significant impact over time. Complaining is contagious, and dissatisfaction spreads. Employees who lack motivation often do not have the patience and energy needed to deal with customers or clients. They may not represent your organization positively to individuals outside through failing to follow through with commitments, not offering suitable explanations and not investing time or energy in satisfying requests. This can lead to a reputation for poor service that is difficult to turn around.

How to Encourage Motivation

Each job contains both task and social characteristics in different proportions. Research has repeatedly confirmed that jobs that provide higher levels of the following specific task characteristics are more motivating:

- The opportunity to complete an entire piece of work from the beginning to the end provides a level of task identity.
- The opportunity to use a broader selection of skills on a variety of tasks provides a level of skill variety.
- The level of impact that the work has on others defines the task significance.
- The level of discretion in determining how work is done and scheduling the work defines the level of autonomy.
- The level of feedback that is provided, specifically information regarding an individual's performance.

Similarly, jobs that include social roles that provide opportunities for the development of strong interpersonal relationships either within the organization or with people outside, including customers, clients, and suppliers, have been shown to be related to high levels of motivation. These relationships allow individuals to both give support to others and to receive it from them (Barrick et al., 2013).

The interaction of the characteristics of a job and an individual's preferences will result in the motivation to work hard at something that is personally meaningful. For example, an individual who has a high need for communication in his or her personal goals will be more highly motivated by a job that provides a higher degree of interdependence among coworkers. The experience of meaningfulness that results is a combination of feelings of significance and usefulness at work.

A colleague described it to me like this:

> Even after my new manager started and it was obvious that we were not going to see eye-to-eye, I continued to really enjoy my work because of the time that I spent with our clients and helping to find solutions to their problems. Getting to help them and seeing that they really appreciated the things that I was able to do for them motivated me to do my best work. Since most of this work was out of the manager's sight, I was able to do my best for the clients. When my job was changed and I had to work in the office, writing policies and reviewing documents all of the time, there was no satisfaction left. Pretty soon I was using up all my sick leave, and when that was gone, I decided to leave. I couldn't see that I was doing any good.

If people who have a high need for status are placed in leadership positions, they are likely to feel a sense of significance and usefulness when managing multiple projects and setting expectations for others. This will result in their bringing more energy, dedication, and absorption to their role, that is, they are highly motivated. Note that this does not refer to how successful they are, but simply that they have found the right combination of personal goals and job characteristics to motivate them to work hard. This is described as a concordant work situation. A discordant work situation, on the other hand, occurs when there is a lack of alignment between a person's goals and the characteristics of his or her job. For example, individuals who have a high need for autonomy but who are in jobs where there is little discretion and the opportunity to complete only a small part of a larger task will not perceive their work as meaningful. In this situation, it is unlikely that they would be motivated because of the need to constantly direct their energy and attention to overcoming the limitations of a job that does not support their goals. Over time they become demotivated, leading to them becoming frustrated, worn out, and emotionally drained (Barrick et al., 2013).

One of the most confusing things for a manager to address when considering motivation is that most of the conditions for motivation are based on individual perceptions. Research has shown that subjective perceptions of job characteristics have two to three times the power of objective characteristics when predicting how employees will react (Barrick et al., 2013). These perceptions are shaped by the individual's goals. For example, a person who has a high need for autonomy may perceive that his or her work allows for very little discretion, while a person with a low need for autonomy might perceive that the same job has an undesirable amount of independence.

The question of money invariably arises during discussions of employee motivation. Individuals talk about losing their motivation when they reach the top of their pay scales and of feeling unappreciated when they are not paid as well as others; pay equity is therefore a frequent issue in the library and information environment as it is often interpreted as representing the amount of respect that an individual experiences.

Does money actually motivate people to work harder? Traditionally, researchers believed that if you paid employees more when their work supported organizational goals, then they would work harder toward those goals. Money, if it motivates people, would be a source of external motivation. Extrinsic rewards, like money, do result in motivation, but the quality and persistence of the work is not as good as if it resulted from intrinsic motivation. Activities that are not, in and of themselves, interesting may require a level of external motivation like pay in order for people to engage in them.

One of the factors that influences whether pay motivates employees is organizational justice. In particular, two components of justice are shown to have a significant impact on the relationship between compensation and motivation: distributive justice and procedural justice. Perceptions of distributive justice reflect the belief that their pay is related to their contribution to the organization; perceptions of procedural justice reflect the belief that a fair process was used to determine the amount of pay and that they had influence over the outcome (Olafsen, Halvari, Forest, & Deci, 2015). Perceptions of justice in compensation have a significantly greater effect on levels of motivation than the actual amount of money that an employee receives. This should serve as a reminder to management that, even in time of economic stress, how compensation is determined and allocated is an important component of a motivated workforce. Meeting people's needs for distributive and procedural justice will provide a level of motivation by making them feel valued and appreciated.

Employees who experience a positive and supportive work environment report feeling motivated regardless of their actual level of compensation. Pay plays a greater role in an unsupportive work environment, perhaps because it is viewed as compensation for an unpleasant work climate, as explained by the need for distributive justice (Olafsen et al., 2015). Procedural justice plays a significant role in the link between pay and motivation. When a high level of procedural justice is perceived, employees feel that they are more autonomous and more competent, and this leads to a higher level of intrinsic motivation. Since research has demonstrated that intrinsic motivation has a much greater and lasting impact on employee motivation, it is clear that the processes used to determine and allocate pay are extremely important. If managers have no control over how pay is allocated, they need, at the very least, to ensure that employees understand the process.

Motivation and Employee Engagement

The characteristics of a job that promote higher levels of motivation also nurture employee engagement. Sufficient resources to meet expectations foster learning and development and personal growth, which support higher levels of engagement. Feedback and supervisor support, while increasing levels of motivation, also reduce the potential negative effects of workloads, help to prevent burnout, and support engagement.

Work that is challenging, allows staff members to complete something that is meaningful, and supports an outcome that they value leads to higher levels of intrinsic motivation and creates an environment that supports employee engagement.

ORGANIZATIONAL CITIZENSHIP BEHAVIOR: WHAT IT IS

The term *organizational citizenship behavior* (OCB) is used to describe contributions that employees make to their organization that fall outside of their specific job requirements. They reflect ways in which an employee contributes discretionary effort to be a good citizen of the workplace. OCBs may include activities that support the social environment in the workplace, support coworkers in the achievement of their expectations, or support the organization outside of the work environment. Since these are not part of an employee's mandated responsibilities, these activities cannot be encouraged with the same strategies that support success in meeting job requirements. In general, OCB is promoted by a positive organizational climate and inhibited by an unfavorable organizational climate. To be considered OCB, an action must have three characteristics: it must go beyond formal job requirements, it must be discretionary, and it must benefit the organization.

Organizations rely on OCBs even if they are not aware of it. The behaviors generally fall into three separate categories: those directed toward an individual, those directed toward customers, and those directed toward the organization itself. Behaviors directed toward individuals demonstrate altruism and courtesy, those directed toward customers include conscientiousness and loyalty, and those directed toward the organization demonstrate conscientiousness, sportsmanship, and civic virtue (Podsakoff, Whiting, Podsakoff, & Blume, 2009).

Altruism is the desire to help others while not expecting to be rewarded. In the workplace, an example is volunteering to help a coworker finish a task or being willing to trade shifts to allow a coworker to attend a family function. Altruism supports good interpersonal relationships among employees. It also has a practical effect by reducing stress on other employees who may need a little bit of support in order to avoid becoming overwhelmed. Altruism also includes participating in activities that support others' efforts to maintain their health and well-being, such as joining a walking group and praising others when they are successful. In libraries, volunteering to be a mentor to a new colleague has been identified as an example of altruistic behavior that benefits the organization by advancing the career of the individual being mentored (Peng, Hwang, & Wong, 2010) and increasing his or her ability to contribute to organizational goals. When altruism is directed at customers, it refers to going an extra step to help a person in a face-to-face or online situation.

Courtesy is expected in the workplace, but it is generally not explicitly defined as part of a job description. It can be defined as a level of consideration toward other people. This can be as simple as asking about personal issues that a coworker has previously raised or checking on progress with a task. It also involves sharing a certain amount of information with coworkers, such as when you might be absent from work. Improving the level of courtesy at work has positive outcomes in terms of interpersonal interactions among employees. Simple actions such as greeting coworkers have a cumulative positive impact on the workplace but are not part of formal expectations.

When discussing OCB, sportsmanship is defined as refraining from exhibiting negative behavior when something goes wrong, no matter how much you might feel like slamming the door or complaining. In a work context, this refers to not complaining about work or reacting negatively to work-related surprises such as schedule changes or new procedures. It is easy to see that reducing the level of complaining in a workplace has positive effects on interpersonal relationship. This is particularly important given the contagious nature of complaining: once one person starts to complain, others are likely to join in.

Conscientiousness, in discussions of OCB, refers to behavior that demonstrates self-control and self-discipline and goes beyond the minimum requirements of a job. For example, coming to work on time is a job requirement, but being willing to shift break times in order to get work completed is a form of conscientiousness. An example of conscientiousness is persisting with extra effort beyond the level that is required and going over and above expectations. It can also include taking extra steps that will prevent additional work or problems for coworkers. When referring to customers, it refers to taking extra steps to ensure that they are satisfied and making sure that they are offered all of the services that are available to them.

Conscientiousness also includes managing one's own learning. As the library and information environment faces ongoing change, learning new skills has become an important component of success. An individual can choose to increase the quality of his or her work through self-managed learning or by participating actively in mandated training. While it is true that a supervisor can offer, or even mandate, training or professional development programs, it is impossible to force an employee to learn. Therefore, the willingness to participate actively in learning and professional development is a discretionary behavior, over and above job requirements. In a changing work environment, the willingness to learn new skills is a crucial aspect of success. Therefore, conscientiousness, or lack thereof, will have a noticeable impact on the success of change processes.

The final component of OCB is called civic virtue and refers to how well a person supports his or her organization outside of his or her official responsibilities. This includes speaking positively about the organization to family and friends or signing up for organization-sponsored events such as charity walks. Civic virtue builds a sense of community, which has been shown to contribute to both job performance and job satisfaction. One example of civic virtue is promoting library events on a person's personal Facebook page. This also includes providing feedback and making suggestions that will improve services or products (Dekas, Bauer, Welle, Kurkoski, & Sullivan, 2013). When referring to customers, civic virtue refers to promoting the organization and its image to customers in a positive way.

Why OCB Motivation Is Good for Employees

Although OCBs are not required by the organization, there is a great deal of evidence to show that they affect supervisors' evaluations of performance. This may be because managers recognize that OCBs carried out by employees make their jobs easier and choose to encourage these through better performance evaluations or more organizational rewards (Podsakoff et al., 2009). Because these behaviors are discretionary, managers may use them as a proxy to estimate how focused employees are on the success of the organization, and how committed they are to the accomplishment of its goals. Managers tend to feel positive about employees who exhibit OCBs, and this may influence performance ratings unintentionally. Employees who are observed taking on OCBs typically receive more positive performance ratings and more recommendations for rewards. In many cases, OCB is more strongly related with performance evaluations than is actual job performance.

Some evidence that OCBs are good for employees is that employees who exhibit higher levels of OCB are less likely to leave the organization, either by looking for another job or by high levels of absenteeism. This behavior also builds stronger interpersonal relationships and group cohesiveness, both of which have shown to be sources of managing stress at work by contributing to improved psychological well-being.

Why OCB Is Good for Organizations

OCB contributes to increased success in meeting organizational goals through increased levels of performance (Randhawa & Kaur, 2015). It appears to do this by increasing productivity as employees help each other through difficult times and make efforts to contribute new ideas and solve problems that are not strictly part of their assigned work. Increased levels of organizational behavior contribute to the perception that a particular organization is a good place to work and assist in attracting and retaining the best employees. Organizations that experience higher levels of OCB are able to adapt more effectively to changes in the environment as employees are willing to go beyond formal roles to make things work (Peng et al., 2010).

The effect of OCBs is particularly significant in organizations that provide services rather than goods, which includes most library and information environments. Customer satisfaction is higher in organizations with higher levels of OCB, demonstrated by increased customer loyalty, positive customer impressions of the organization, and a reduced likelihood that they will complain to others when problems arise (Payne & Webber, 2006). This positive effect on the quality of customer service is even more effective with recurring customers, making it an important consideration in the library and information environment. This effect is enhanced by increased levels of autonomy for employees, empowering employees, increasing responsibilities, and maximizing autonomy.

How to Encourage OCB

The organizational climate is the most significant characteristic of an organization that predicts the level of OCB. Within the climate, the factors that have the most impact are support from supervisors, performance feedback, clarity of organizational goals, level of autonomy, workload pressure, and level of participation in decision making (Randhawa & Kaur, 2015).

Support from supervisors gives employees a higher level of confidence in completing job expectations that spills over into increased confidence in doing other things in the workplace. A supportive supervisor leads to a good overall impression of the organization, resulting in a willingness to accept the organization's goals, and support them, even outside of the workplace. This support of organizational goals increases employees' willingness to help others to achieve these goals, a form of OCB. Having clearly articulated goals also increases the likelihood that employees will help coworkers as they are more aware of the expected outcome of tasks.

Perceptions of whether or not the supervisor is listening have been shown to have a considerable effect on many employee outcomes, including OCB. Listening is an important signal of managerial openness that encourages productive communication. Employees who believe that they are listened to are more likely to disclose information and experience a safe atmosphere where they can speak openly. Active listening supports perceptions of respect, justice, and trust (Lloyd, Boer, Keller, & Voelpel, 2015). Supervisors who are good listeners create a positive work environment and encourage positive attitudes toward the organization and the work that needs to be done. Supervisors who are perceived as poor listeners increase the risk of emotional exhaustion and eventually burnout, as employees believe that it is not safe to reveal difficulties or express emotions, which limits opportunities to resolve problems early.

As the perceived level of workload increases, OCB decreases. This is a result of increased time and effort being focused on assigned tasks, leaving little left over to assist others or make voluntary contributions in the workplace. Employees feel that they have little discretion about their assigned tasks, so they reduce their effort where they can (Randhawa & Kaur, 2015).

Increased participation in decision making also leads to an increase in OCBs in addition to a greater focus on assigned job expectations. This may be because people generally have a higher level of commitment to decisions that they have been part of and are therefore willing to expend some of their discretionary effort in making them successful. Perceptions of fairness also have a significant impact on the likelihood that an individual will engage in OCBs. This includes the recognition of OCBs in performance evaluations as an indicator of distributive justice. Since these discretionary behaviors have a positive impact on organizational success, it is both appropriate and desirable that they be recognized in this way (Podsakoff et al., 2009).

Job satisfaction is associated with higher levels of OCB, so strategies that increase job satisfaction have the added benefit of increasing OCB. The links between job satisfaction and OCB in librarians are enhanced when employees perceive that they have a greater level of autonomy (Peng et al., 2010). Providing staff members with a high degree of discretion over how their work is carried out, encouraging innovation and new approaches, and making allowances for failure all will have a beneficial effect on both job satisfaction and OCB. Increasing levels of participation in decision making through interactions between managers and staff members and encouraging employees to contribute their ideas also support both job satisfaction and OCB (Peng et al., 2010).

The impact of OCBs is stronger with recurring customers; they appreciate the extra effort offered by employees. Increasing levels of autonomy and empowering customer service employees to make decisions that benefit customers increase job satisfaction as well as OCBs. OCBs are critical to good service as it is difficult to predict customer requests, and staff members need to demonstrate flexibility to provide customer satisfaction. More satisfied employees consistently demonstrate the intention to provide the best quality service, and these attitudes are contagious and spill over to the customers (Payne & Webber, 2006). Staff members have the opportunity to demonstrate loyalty to the organization by promoting its image to customers and speaking positively about organizational management and policies.

Organizational change brings new stresses to organizations and employees (Sharif & Scandura, 2014). Management is often challenged when having to introduce decisions that may be difficult or unpopular. There is evidence that if employees feel that their manager is ethical, they are more likely to support the change and exhibit OCB that is of benefit during the change process. The perception of ethical leadership is based on management actions that include modeling desired behavior by making ethical decisions, rewarding ethical behavior in others, and being seen to deal with unethical behavior.

Management transparency is an essential component of ethical leadership and is supported by engaging employees in decision making that allows them to voice opinions, including negative ones. During periods of change, this creates a greater sense of control, even when their input does not form part of the final decision. Employees who are involved and knowledgeable about the change that is occurring demonstrate a greater level of confidence in management reliability (Sharif & Scandura, 2014) and therefore experience a sense of psychological safety that supports OCB.

A POTENTIAL DOWNSIDE TO OCB

While there are clearly many benefits to high levels of OCB, like many other things in life, things can go wrong if it is taken too far. A critical look at OCBs shows that in some cases, employees are engaging in this behavior not from a sense of altruism or generosity but as a result of boredom with their regular work or the potential for manipulation of a supervisor's impression of their work. If OCBs become the norm for the organization, employees may feel the need to perform at ever-increasing levels in order to be seen as going the extra mile. This can result in role ambiguity, role overload, and work-family conflict as a result of increasing pressure to add additional work to their assigned workload (Bolino, Klotz, Turnley, & Harvey, 2013).

OCB and Employee Engagement

A demonstrated association between OCB and employee engagement is particularly noticeable in OCBs that are directed at the organization. Since engagement is about the willingness to bring enthusiasm and passion to work to help the employer succeed, it goes beyond the simple requirements of meeting the expectations of the job. The additional contributions made by an engaged employee typically include OCBs.

EMPLOYEE WELL-BEING: WHAT IT IS

Well-being is described as having three components: a general sense of satisfaction with life, feeling that one's moods are generally pleasant, and that one's life is generally aligned with your own sense of purpose. It often includes positive relationships with other people, mastery of skills, and a level of self-acceptance. It is a subjective measure that goes beyond having sufficient economic resources and objective issues such as workplace safety.

Employee well-being (EWB) refers to extent that employees are generally satisfied with their jobs, and frequently experience positive emotions at work. It includes the quality of experiences at work, negative effects such as stress or burnout, and an overall personal assessment of how work experiences interact with the rest of their lives. This equates to an evaluation of whether their lives are meaningful and has value.

EWB goes beyond physical and mental health and looks at issues of the quality of life. In Western society, it also goes beyond economic issues, and it is likely that awareness of EWB and its relevance for management will grow in developing countries alongside economic development. As people are increasingly able to meet their economic needs, they are inclined to be more aware of their general levels of happiness and the fulfillment of their social and psychological needs at work (Ilies, Aw, & Pluut, 2015).

While individual personality traits certainly play a part in EWB, organizational factors also make a significant contribution. While extremely high demands in a job can have a negative effect of EWB, research shows that managers can overcome these by ensuring that employees have the optimum level of control over their work, the resources that they need to do the job, and that there is a level of social support provided by supervisors and coworkers.

Why Well-Being Is Good for Employees

EWB has a significant impact on the overall quality of people's lives because of the amount of time that they spend at work. Employees who experience a higher sense of well-being enjoy better health, fewer hospital visits, better job performance ratings, and many other benefits. They experience lower levels of depression and are less likely to abuse alcohol or drugs. EWB spills over into other areas of people's lives, such as relationships with their families and friends (Ilies et al., 2015).

Individuals have a limited amount of resources to fulfill the demands of daily life. Job demands that cannot be met lead to a level of conflict and exhaustion that often results in work-family conflict, which increases the level of stress that the individual is experiencing. This then turns into a downward spiral. On the other hand, an employee who experiences a high level of well-being at work as a result of experiences such as development opportunities and a level of autonomy has extra energy to devote to his or her home life.

Why Well-Being Is Good for Organizations

Employees with a higher degree of overall well-being are more productive both in reduced absenteeism and in more fully meeting expectations at work. In general, they experience better health and make less use of organizational health benefits such as disability support. Perceptions of low overall well-being result in lower levels of energy and increased likelihood of being distracted from the task at hand. It is often tied to negative emotions about work resulting in reduced effort or bringing negative emotion into the work group. Individuals who experience higher levels of well-being are more likely to stay with the organization, reducing recruitment and training costs (Sears, Shi, Coberley, & Pope, 2013).

A sense of well-being also leads to employees being willing to go over and above their regular work and contribute discretionary energy to helping coworkers or helping the organization to be more successful through OCBs. One of the interesting outcomes of EWB is a higher level of creativity and innovation. Overall, individuals with a higher sense of personal well-being contribute more in their defined work roles as well as being better organizational citizens in general. They come to work on time and miss less work. Their overall performance is better, which means that the organization can benefit from their skills and energy (Ilies et al., 2015).

Well-being also has a purely financial benefit. In a large sample of employees, the level of overall well-being was correlated with the amount of money that the employer spent on health care, the level of productivity, and the level of staff turnover. This suggests that an investment in EWB has an overall benefit for the organization.

How to Encourage Well-Being

It is an employer's responsibility to provide safe and healthy employment. In the matter of well-being, this clearly goes beyond the traditional issues of a safe workplace and focus on accident prevention. Along with physical safety, an employer is responsible for maintaining an appropriate level of psychological safety by ensuring that there is no bullying or harassment. This understanding of a healthy workplace reflects the World Health Organization's (WHO) definition: "Health is a state of complete physical, mental and social well-being, and not merely the absence of disease or infirmity" (Schulte et al., 2015). WHO then goes on to describe a healthy workplace as one in which employees and managers work together to continually improve the health, safety, and well-being of all employees.

The factors that are outlined by WHO begin with getting commitment and engagement from upper management to integrate issues of EWB into the goals and values of the organization and to provide the necessary resources to support well-being initiatives. It is essential that employees be involved with both the risk assessment and the development of plans to reduce risks. This must go beyond simply being consulted or informed. WHO reminds employers that they have an ethical and legal responsibility to enforce health and safety standards, including those that refer to psychological health and safety. A systematic process will provide for the most comprehensive understanding of what needs to be done to improve the environment for EWB. Like any other organizational change, this requires ongoing commitment in order to be sustainable, and it needs to be integrated into other systems such as performance management (Schulte et al., 2015).

Management style has a significant impact on employees' perceptions of their well-being. Mismanagement has been identified as one of the most significant negative impacts on EWB, resulting in actions that are not good for the organization. For example, family-supportive decisions by a supervisor have been shown to have a direct positive effect on EWB. These are defined as supporting employees who need to meet family commitments, for example, by allowing for flexibility in scheduling (Matthews, Mills, Trout, & English, 2014). Supervisors need to not only understand that they have the autonomy to make these decisions but be trained in how to make them appropriately and be recognized for making them. In other words, family supportiveness needs to be integrated into the organization. It is important that managers feel supported in making these decisions through policy and support from their supervisors. It is interesting to note that family-supportive supervision also has a positive effect on employees who do not have family obligations, as it reinforces the belief that the organization is more employee-friendly.

Other management styles that have been shown to support increased levels of EWB focus on employee participation in decision making, including freedom to express opinions and a level of effective communication between individuals and their supervisors (Cheng, 2014). In spite of what management articulates and believes, employees often feel excluded from participating in management decisions, which is particularly frustrating for those who are interested in progressing to management roles. This is often interpreted as management not being interested in employees' opinions or wishing to keep all of the power for themselves.

Employee wellness programs also have a positive effect on well-being. Focus on areas such as stress management, living with diversity, wellness, and programs for personal growth have all been shown to be effective. Studies in the United States, however, suggest that lack of employee participation in these programs limits their effectiveness. Only about 24% of employees reported participating in employer-sponsored wellness activities (Tinney, 2015). Reasons for nonparticipation include not believing that they are needed, not having time, or that the location or schedule is inconvenient.

Some suggestions for increasing the participation in wellness programs include providing rewards and recognition for participation and ensuring that managers model participation in programs. Management participation sends several positive messages: that these programs are part of the culture of the organization and that participation is important.

Relationship with Employee Engagement

Well-being is a bigger concept than engagement, but the two are closely related. Highly engaged employees experience higher levels of well-being, but well-being has a much greater spillover effect into employees' personal lives (Shimazu, Schaugeli, Kamiyama, & Kawakami, 2015). Family-supportive supervision, for example, allows employees to manage their family obligations, resulting in more time and energy for work, which increase both engagement and well-being.

REFLECTION QUESTIONS

The questions below can be used for personal reflection or to stimulate discussion in staff groups.

1. Think about a time when you were not highly motivated at work. The following situations have all been identified as having the potential to reduce motivation. Did any of them apply in your situation? Then consider whether or not any of them are the responsibility of you as an individual employee; in other words how much control do you have over your own level of motivation?

   (a) Micromanagement or lack of autonomy

   (b) Lack of progress toward expectations

   (c) Lack of confidence in supervisors or management

   (d) Lack of consequences for poor performance

   (e) Poor communication about the purpose of tasks

   (f) Unpleasant coworkers

   (g) Boredom

2. When you think about OCBs in your organization, do they seem to be discretionary, or are they expected? Some organizations recognize and reward employees for going beyond the expected and in this way encourage OCBs. This can be demotivating for employees who lack the time, energy, or other resources to commit to OCBs. Can you think of ways in which OCBs are beneficial in your situation and ways in which they may have more negative consequences?

5

Integrating Strategies and Policies to Improve the Workplace Climate

Many individual differences affect employee motivation and engagement, including the role that work plays within an individual's life. Studies of happiness, however, point to the important role that employment plays. Many psychologists believe that being employed, whether paid or not, is an innate need for all people (Robinson, Kennedy, & Harmon, 2012). Some people do not choose to invest themselves in their work but use their employment to support their real interests, which provide them with their sense of accomplishment and satisfaction. These interests may include community service or hobbies. Nonetheless, an improvement in a workplace climate that nurtures motivation and engagement will have positive impacts on both employees and the organization.

After an organization or a manager has had the chance to reflect on the climate in their workplace and is interested in making changes, the next step is to implement new strategies. One of the most challenging issues for managers, and most frustrating for employees, is ensuring that all of the strategies, policies, and guidelines are integrated so that there are clear directions and they do not contradict each other. Employee engagement is affected by both contextual and interpersonal influences, and this chapter brings together several of these into an integrated approach.

Well-integrated policies and strategies are part of a healthy workplace climate. Simply developing good policies will not have the desired effect if they are not consistently enacted and if they are not aligned with each other. Conflicting directions, documents, policies, and practices create levels of ambiguity that are contrary to the environment required to support employee engagement. Ambiguity has negative outcomes on employees' connections to the organization and leads employees to question management's competence and effectiveness. Clarity supports motivation, commitment, and engagement.

Policies and practices must be integrated both vertically and horizontally. Vertical integration implies that all policies and practices contribute to the goals and directions of the organization. Horizontal integration implies that all policies and practices are congruent with each other. For example, job advertisements that identify innovation as one of the requirements of a job may support a goal of finding new ways of offering service, demonstrating vertical integration. If, however, the reward system does not support innovation, there is no horizontal integration.

Policies and practices are both formal and informal. Their intent is to ensure that all of the organization's resources are utilized in an optimal way to contribute to the accomplishment of organizational goals. Human resources are one of the most significant assets that an organization has, as they represent the skill and innovation that is available to the organization. An integrated approach to human resource management (HRM) aligns with organizational factors and the external environment and includes broad-based accountability for all managers and supervisors. HRM is therefore required to be not a set of rules or transactions but a strategy that is a significant component of organizational success.

A colleague shared this story with me:

> I was so excited when I got this job. The interviewing committee told me that one of the strongest parts of my resume was my connections with groups in the community, and that they felt this would bring value to the library. I felt that I had something unique to bring and that it would strengthen the library's ties with the community and that would improve both service and the library's reputation. When I had my first performance appraisal, I was shocked when my supervisor said that I had to focus more on the library, and stop worrying so much about other community groups. When I tried to discuss this with her, pointing out that these community groups were part of our service mandate, she replied that they weren't paying me and the library was. I was so deflated, and I felt that someone had lied to me.

MISSIONS, VISIONS, AND OTHER PLANNING DOCUMENTS

A starting place for integration is the mission of the organization. It needs to articulate what the organization is intending to accomplish, how this is going to come about, and what the benefit is for the community. Whether this is accomplished by a mission statement or some other document, it is the basis for creating a healthy and supportive environment. It defines a framework that informs employees of the values and goals of the organization and how their work supports the organization's success. These documents should articulate the employer's commitment to a workplace that is healthy and safe, both physically and psychologically.

For any planning documents, including the mission of the organization, there are several factors that have an impact on how successful it will be. They include employees' perception of the quality of the statement and how it was developed, whether the organization's leaders model the values of the statements, and how clear the statements are (Desmidt, 2016). While it saves time initially, simply adopting or adapting from other organizations fails to support positive employee perceptions.

What makes goals attractive and persuasive for employees? Clarity is essential. Unfortunately, rather than being clear and compelling, many mission statements and subsequent planning documents are ambiguous, containing phrases like "the highest possible quality" without agreement on what "highest possible" or "quality" mean when they become part of an employee's understanding of their work. The more ambiguous the statement or plan, the less it is effective in engaging employees' interest.

As well as being a public statement about the organization, mission statements and planning documents must be seen to be an active part of the daily life of the organization. If employees are to use these documents to guide their relationship with the organization, including their commitment and engagement, managers must be seen to model behavior that supports the mission and plan. Otherwise, they create hypocrisy, cynicism, and a loss of credibility. Employees will tend to do what they see managers doing regardless of what policies and guidelines require.

When the mission of the organization is clear and unambiguous, and employees can see how their efforts support the directions of the organization, they are more likely to see their work as being meaningful and to expend more effort in supporting organizational goals (Desmidt, 2016). A mission statement and planning documents that are delivered top-down within an organization are unlikely to be perceived by all employees in the same way, reducing their value in providing direction. This can be resolved in increasing the level of employee participation in their development.

Prosocial values are an integral part of the training, professional identity, and socialization of many people who work in the library and information environment. Individuals who perceive that they are making a contribution to the community through their work experience more positive emotions, which support higher levels of employee engagement. Thus, the values component of planning documents has a significant impact on this workforce. Employees who are able to see that their work contributes to the accomplishment of valued goals experience higher levels of meaningfulness in their work, which also supports employee engagement. It is important, therefore, to ensure that employees are clear about how their work contributes to the benefit of the communities served (Freeney & Fellenz, 2013).

Participation

Perceptions of participation are an important factor in positive employee outcomes. Employees who believe that they are able to effectively communicate with management in a variety of ways demonstrate higher levels of commitment, organizational citizenship behavior, and engagement. When employees believe that their contribution is valued by management, they respond with positive attitudes and behaviors.

Employee voice is defined as the way in which employees can contribute their ideas and opinions about what goes on in an organization, either through formal or informal systems. Specifically, it refers to ways in which employees are able to speak up about organizational changes or improvements, even when others disagree with them, and the responses that they get. Employees who believe that they are able to influence decisions demonstrate higher levels of organizational commitment as well as increasing their level of discretionary effort, both of which benefit the organization. A sense of being valued is one of the drivers of engagement, and the ability to voice concerns and have them heard by management is one of the indicators that an employee is valued.

When employees believe that senior management hears and values their contributions, they develop a greater sense of trust in the organization's leaders. This level of trust increases the likelihood that they will meet their workplace commitments, both now and in the future. Managerial processes have a significant effect on levels of engagement, and many of employees' perceptions of an organization's management come from their interactions with their direct supervisors. This does not mean that the supervisor, representing the organization, always acts on their suggestions but simply that they are listened to and accepted respectfully.

Middle managers and supervisors have a significant role in translating organizational goals into unit and individual directions. Supervisors who adopt a philosophy that their main role is to support and serve their staff contribute to a highly engaged workforce. Of particular importance is the supervisor's role in providing information. A reciprocal relationship develops in which the supervisor who provides information is likely to encourage employees to offer information, which in turn enables the supervisor to be more successful. Managers can always explain to staff members how decisions are being made, particularly those where there is no opportunity for staff input, as well as provide as much information as possible about timing and implementation. This transparency helps employees to understand where and when they are able and welcome to participate. Middle managers also have responsibility for communicating reactions and concerns about decisions to upper management, and in particular, the impact of decisions on units and individuals.

Employees who perceive themselves as being able to freely offer suggestions and opinions are more engaged. Trust in senior management and healthy relationships with supervisors both support this kind of positive communication (Rees, Alfes, & Gatenby, 2013). Participation in decision making helps employees to achieve their work goals, which contributes to a sense of mastery and competence, leading to higher levels of engagement. It also reduces stress as employees are able to articulate concerns and make suggestions about how work can best be carried out.

The Role of Supervisor

The role of supervisors or line managers is fundamental in understanding how employees perceive and respond to an organization's human resource management (HRM) policies and practices. They are the ones who are responsible for ensuring that policies and practices are implemented in the way that the organization intended and that employees understand them.

Supervisors have a significant impact on levels of engagement. Those who are able to develop trusting relationships with employees comprising open communication, sharing information, and providing support will promote higher levels of employee engagement. If they are able to act as a conduit for feedback to higher levels of management and create an environment of effective interpersonal relationships, this impact will be strengthened.

As well as the traditional elements of supervisor training, some additional elements can increase levels of employee engagement such as:

- An understanding of the role that the supervisor plays in translating information about the organization and about policies and procedures to their staff and how staff use this to attribute characteristics to senior management. This includes modeling the mission, values, and other statements of the organization.

- Skills that support two-way communication and the importance of open and noncritical communication for both sharing information and for supporting the employees' perception that they are valued. This includes skills in delivering unpopular information and conflict management.

- The role of the supervisor in creating and maintaining a positive environment in which employees are willing to contribute their effort and energy toward meeting organizational goals. This includes the consistent implementation of HRM practices and a clear understanding of the role of organizational justice in the workplace. Managers' goals and appraisals must reflect these issues and include an assessment of their management style and its effectiveness.

Supervisors have a significant role in developing employees through their belief in the capability of the employee, allowing risk and experimentation, reinforcing strengths, creating opportunities for improvement, and allowing for the implementation and practice of new skills (Chaudhary, Rangnekar, & Barua, 2011). Additionally, they play a major role in influencing whether new learning is utilized in the workplace by ensuring that there is an opportunity to apply new skills, developing goals for the use of skills, and providing feedback and encouragement (Martin, 2010).

Transformational leadership skills have been demonstrated to be particularly effective as a way of promoting employee engagement. Therefore, this is a skill set that needs to be incorporated into supervisors' and managers' expectations and evaluation, predicated on the organization providing training for all managers. The important components of transformational leadership are individualized consideration, intellectual stimulation, inspirational motivation, and idealized influence. Individualized consideration refers to the degree to which leaders attend to the needs and concerns of employees and recognize their abilities and contribution. Intellectual stimulation describes the extent to which leaders are able to challenge their own assumptions and encourage employees to explore new perspectives. Unexpected situations are interpreted as opportunities for learning rather than problems. Inspirational motivation describes the ability to communicate an engaging vision for the future and provide a sense of optimism about it. Finally, idealized influence provides a model for high ethical standards and thus gains respect and trust (Breevaart et al., 2014). This is clearly a departure from many traditional management styles.

Communication

While everyone agrees that communication is a good thing to have in an organization, and many employees complain about the communication in their workplace, management rarely successfully addresses improvement in communication. This stems from a lack of understanding about why communication is essential, and how it can be managed.

Good communication helps employees to achieve their work goals as they understand both what they are supposed to do and how it contributes to the overall success of the organization. It reduces role ambiguity and allows employees to devote their energies to appropriate activities. Employees are more likely to become immersed in their work when they perceive that it has value to the organization, and this contributes to higher levels of engagement. Staff members who perceive that they do not get sufficient and timely communication are more likely to become disillusioned and stressed, resulting in reduced engagement (Shantz, Alfes, & Arevshatian, 2016).

Good communication is the keystone of transparency and has a significant impact on the degree to which employees trust supervisors and management. Strong internal communications build commitment and lead to higher levels of employee engagement. Trust is developed through appropriate, clear, and timely information that allows for an open relationship. The credibility of management is questioned when communications appear to be distorted, reducing the level of respect that employees have and eventually reducing their engagement.

Communications between management and employees has been shown to contribute to superior customer service as well-informed employees can become advocates for the organization's role in solving customer problems. Good communication also improves productivity by streamlining processes and encouraging collaboration.

Research suggests that an integrated communications approach, with a consistent message to employees as well as to the external community, is the most effective. In practice, however, many organizations see internal communication as a function of supervisors and the human resource department and external communication as a function of the marketing department, leading to inconsistent timing and content of messages.

Internal communication is interpreted as a reflection of the level of management's commitment to build relationships among all of the parts of an organization. It should provide employees with the information that they need not only to do their job but also to establish connections between different pieces of information. It is one of the tools that reduces the level of friction during periods of organizational change. Timely, accurate, and relevant information helps employees to feel less vulnerable (Mishra, Boynton, & Mishra, 2014).

As well as organization-wide communication strategies, it is important to consider the role that face-to-face communication plays in building trust and employee engagement. Because it is a combination of communication and interaction, it provides visual and verbal cues that support or undermine the validity of the information. It is considered to be more reliable than written communication when there is a match between the message and the other cues. This means that organizations should pay a great deal of attention to the communication skills of those who interact frequently with their employees, generally middle managers or supervisors. It is also important to ensure that those people actually have enough time for face-to-face conversations.

Senior managers need to also consider how they communicate as this provides a model of desirable behavior throughout the organization. Paying constant attention to openly aligning decisions to the goals of the organization and showing that appropriate procedures are being followed for decision making will set a standard for middle managers to follow. Two-way communication at the top level reduces cynicism, which is contrary to employee engagement. Listening to employees reminds them that they are important and are valued by the organization.

Human Resource Practices

HRM policies and practices that lead to high engagement are broadly focused around three areas: employee skills, motivation, and empowerment. It is important to remember that whatever was intended by management, it is the employees' understanding and perceptions of these that drive their behavior. Research suggests that alignment between intention, implementation, and perception is relatively poor, largely due to levels of variability in implementation (Alfes, Truss, Soane, Rees, & Gatenby, 2013).

Recruitment activities must be integrated with all of the other components of the organization, because it is a major element in the development of the psychological contract. Potential employees understand that their experience of the organization through job advertisements, selection processes, and job offers shapes their expectations of their future employment. For example, if an organization values service to the community, this value should be repeated through all steps of the recruitment process. Determining a level of alignment between individual values and organizational values allows employees to pursue goals that are both meaningful for themselves, leading to a high level of engagement, and beneficial to the organization.

Human resource practices are often the clearest indication that an employee gets of the enacted values of the organization, which may not align with the articulated values. Again, this speaks to the important role that the supervisor plays; his or her behavior will be perceived to reflect the real values of the organization. For optimal impact, human resource messages should be distinctive, consistent, and directed at producing a high level of consensus among employees about the types of behavior that are appropriate and expected as an employee of this particular organization.

Performance appraisal systems must be aligned both with the overall goals and plans of the organization and with all of the other human resource policies and practices. They must recognize and reward behavior in accordance with the effort expended and the successes achieved in order to maximize perceptions of distributive justice. The process must be as close to the same as possible for all employees in order to support procedural justice.

Training and Development

Job resources help employees to achieve their work expectations and reduce negative outcomes such as burnout. Training is one form of job resource. It provides employees with the necessary skills to carry out their work successfully, and as they feel more competent, they will be inspired by their work, leading to increased employee engagement. Development opportunities also have a positive impact as they build morale and support personal and career opportunities. They have been shown to reduce emotional exhaustion and increase the level of energy that employees are willing to devote to their work (Shantz et al., 2016).

One of the keys to keeping employees engaged is to provide opportunities for them to continue to develop their skills and knowledge throughout their careers. In particular, opportunities that are aligned with their individual goals and aspirations will engage their attention and create a sense of obligation to the organization that will be rewarded with greater productivity as well as enhanced engagement. While training tends to focus on current needs, development contributes to flexibility in the future and helps employees to perceive that their organization values them in the long term.

The purpose of training and development is to increase the level of perceived self-efficacy of each employee, which describes their belief that they can perform successfully to meet the expectations of their jobs (Chaudhary et al., 2011). Higher levels of perceived self-efficacy are related to higher levels of employee engagement as well as successful organizational change. Self-efficacy is also significant in determining how much effort people will put into an activity, how long they will persevere under difficult circumstances, and how resilient they will be if things go wrong.

Employees have a general perception about the developmental climate within an organization that includes both formal and informal training opportunities, support, feedback, and the ability to use new skills. It extends beyond their experience and includes the experiences of coworkers whom they observe, including how fairly opportunities are made available. A more positive perception of the development climate has a significant impact on the level of employee engagement across an organization.

Social Support from Coworkers

Social support refers to both verbal and nonverbal support from others that reduces uncertainty and provides feedback. One of the most undervalued and understudied forms of support in the workplace is that provided by coworkers. It may be as straightforward as providing information, such as helping a new coworker find supplies, or as complex as providing emotional support when a coworker has a difficult experience with a client. Collegial support is of particular value during times of organizational change as a source of shared information and emotional support. Peers are also an important source of mentoring, which allows individuals to seek alternative responses to challenging situations.

Peer support has a significant positive impact on the implementation of new skills that are developed through training programs. Coworkers provide the motivation to try out new skills and provide feedback and recognition. Research suggests that it is more important than supervisor behavior in support of implementation of learning through a closer relationship with the employee. Sharing learning and information allows for improved problem-solving skills and reinforcement of learning. This leads to improved perceptions of competence, which contributes to employee engagement.

Support from coworkers has a significant positive impact on levels of employee engagement. It buffers the requirements of a job that may lead to stress, such as work overload, and supports the individual employee in doing his or her best work through coordination and collaboration with others. Good relationships with coworkers increase the level of positive emotions and protect against exhaustion, particularly in service settings. Peer support has been shown to be particularly useful in overcoming the impact of a negative workplace climate. In contrast, negative interactions with coworkers, such as incivility, have been shown to contribute to chronic stress and burnout.

Job Design

Each job combines levels of demands and control. Demands are the expectations of the job, the outcomes that the employee is expected to work toward, and the ways in which work is to be conducted. The demands placed on the employee include the skills that they bring to the job and the workload. The controls are the balance between the controls exercised by management and those which are delegated to the employee. Jobs with high levels of demands and low levels of control by the employee are characterized as high-strain jobs, contributing to chronic stress and other negative outcomes (De Spiegelaere, Van Gyes, De Witte, & Van Hootegem, 2015). Jobs with high demands and high level of employee control lead to the highest levels of motivation and learning behavior. Higher levels of control over one's own work, autonomy, have been demonstrated to be related to better health as well as more innovative behavior.

Autonomy has a significant impact on the likelihood that an employee will experience a high level of engagement. Factors that contribute to perceived autonomy include the ability to make decisions about how work is done, freedom to plan one's own work, and ability to decide on what work will contribute to the desired outcome. Autonomy allows employees to pursue meaningful work in a way that is congruent with their values. It also allows them to deal with the pressures of time and workload. Employees who are experiencing stress from time and workload and do not have sufficient autonomy to organize their work tend to cope by disengaging (De Spiegelaere et al., 2015).

Employees' perception of autonomy begins with the job description. To allow for the greatest level of autonomy, job descriptions need to contain the essential functions but allow room for discretion in how the employee is to accomplish the tasks that will meet expectations. The less detailed a job description, the greater the employee's perception that they have control over their responsibilities. Employees with good judgment are able to determine how to prioritize their work, set their own deadlines, and set intermediate goals. This operates within the larger framework of outcomes that will support the organization's goals as determined with the supervisor.

For autonomy to be an effective component of an employee's job, it must be enacted consistently. Whatever is implied during the recruitment process and orientation must align with the job description as well as evaluation and reward processes. In this, the role of the supervisor is an essential component, as this is the person who is primarily responsible for the day-to-day perception of autonomy.

Inherent in any organization is the concept that employees need to do the work that is associated with their job. This works well in traditionally stable organizations but does not necessarily result in success in a rapidly changing environment. An alternative view of job design is that jobs will continually be modified as a result of organizational needs. If the concept of employee needs is added to this, it has the potential to enhance engagement. In particular, recognizing that employee goals, interests, and skills evolve, and creating flexibility so that their job expectations can also evolve, will increase the level of meaningfulness. A higher level of meaningfulness results in higher levels of engagement. This evolving job design allows employees to continue to do work that is challenging and varied, with an agreed-upon level of autonomy, and with a good fit between the employee's current skills, needs, and values and the agreed-upon outcomes of the work (Gruman & Saks, 2011).

Ethical Workplace Climate

While organizational culture is a system of shared assumptions, organizational climate is created by the systems, policies, and practices of the organization and explains how employees experience the culture. Culture is ingrained in the behavior of employees and managers and is very difficult to change. Some writers have described it as the personality of the organization. The climate changes regularly and is shaped largely by the management of the organization. In general, human resource policies and practices are developed to influence an employee's perception of climate, with the longer-term goal of encouraging desired behaviors to meet organizational goals. These include activities related to recruitment, training and development, appraisal, and reward systems. These activities all interact to achieve the desired outcome, and they form the climate of the organization. They must be integrated with all of the operational activities of the organization in order to convey the message that they are to be taken seriously (Manroop, Singh, & Ezzedeen, 2014).

An ethical workplace climate occurs when employees believe that ethical behavior is the standard for all decision making throughout the organization. It has a significant impact on the behavior of employees, including how they treat coworkers and customers. A shared ethical climate provides the basis for employees to understand situations and determine how to behave. Ethical climates are not all the same and will vary according to the individual organization. Most researchers identify five significantly different climates: instrumental, caring, independence, law and code based, and rules based. Each of these can be enacted ethically but requires attention to aligning all HRM practices.

Instrumental climates are focused on efficiencies and cost control, and human resource policies will focus on ensuring that recruitment, training, and evaluation practices reflect this. A caring climate focuses on a genuine interest in, and concern for, people's welfare, including both employees and others outside the organization. Again, these values need to be reflected throughout all of the practices of the organization. For example, in this climate, training would address issues such as interpersonal skills, and appraisals would consider how employees support the work of their colleagues. A caring climate has been shown to motivate employees to provide better customer service as well as helping each other. The influence of management is significant in building a caring climate by modeling appropriate behavior through greater collaboration and information sharing.

A third organizational climate is the independence climate that encourages individuals to make decisions based on their own personal values and principles of justice, with minimal influence from the organization. This requires a significant investment in recruitment to ensure that selection is based on ensuring that the employee's values are congruent with that of the organization. Performance management must include expectations for decisions made in the best interest of the organization and its customers. Managers must provide enough leeway for employees to make decisions based on personal values of justice, morality, and respect regardless of organizational context. If all human resource processes are congruent with this climate, the organization invests less in monitoring.

Law and code-based climates are based on the view that decision making relies on external codes such as religion texts, laws, or professional codes of conduct. These tend to occur in highly regulated professional organizations such as engineering and medicine. For a professional organization, this climate increases the perception of legitimacy by customers that results in a more positive image. This would be a challenging climate for a library or information organization due to the proliferation of codes of conduct and the voluntary nature of compliance with them.

Rules-based climate refers to an environment that is based in policies and procedures within the organization that are applied consistently and uniformly. Rules and policies become routine and are embedded in all of the practices of the organization. The rules are specific to the organization and are designed to govern and reinforce specific behaviors that will contribute to the organization's goals. The recruitment process must search for people who are comfortable and will thrive in this climate. Orientation must clearly explain the rules and procedures and motivate new employees to adopt the rules to govern their performance in order to add value to the organization. A rules-based climate emphasizes means rather than ends, so recognition needs to be for compliance. A reward system that recognizes high levels of achievement contravenes this and creates an environment where employees view the rules as barriers to recognition.

It is easy to see how confusion and conflict can occur when there is not a distinct and consistent message to employees. For example, if employees are recruited on the basis of holding values of helping and collaboration, but only individual accomplishment is recognized in the performance appraisal system, they are likely to become confused and disillusioned, resulting in reduced engagement. Many individuals report that the recruitment process implies high levels of judgment and autonomy, but the organizational climate is rules based, causing a breach of their psychological contract (Manroop et al., 2014).

Recruitment

Since the recruitment process is often the first major interaction that an employee has with an organization, it is a useful place for considering management strategies that will nurture employee engagement in the long run. Generally, individuals are at their most engaged at the point at which they decide to join an organization. They are enthusiastic and excited to demonstrate that they can add value and contribute to the organization's goals.

Recruitment strategies provide many of the building blocks of the psychological contract. This is an opportunity for the organization to ensure that the individual knows where the organization is going and how it is evolving to meet the needs of a changing environment. This provides a basis for the decisions that follow. It is also an opportunity to explain to potential employees how success is defined in the organization. The more accurate this explanation is, the more likely that the result will be employees who are a good fit with the organization, both with their personal goals and their skills. Lack of clarity at this stage helps to lead to a breach of the psychological contract and a reduced level of engagement, as the job turns out to be different than was expected.

The recruitment process is an opportunity to demonstrate that yours is an ethical organization. It is a chance to talk about values and to provide evidence that they are enacted and not just talked about. For example, if advertisements state that you are an innovative and nimble organization, what examples can you provide to explain what this actually means in your context? The perception of a mismatch between espoused and actual values decreases the likelihood of engaged employees. An employee who is anticipating working for an innovative organization will be a poor fit for an organization that depends on adherence to strict policies and rules and is unlikely to stay engaged.

As organizations are increasing the level of employee participation in decision making, there is a shift from a transactional model of work, in which an employee does what is asked in exchange for pay, to a relational model of work, in which the employee develops a relationship with the organization that provides benefits to both. The recruitment process allows for the beginning of this relationship by providing an open discussion of these benefits. This relationship, of course, must continue in this way after the employee has joined the organization.

Once a person is hired, the process of engaging him or her does not stop. The person's early experiences are part of a process of socialization as he or she learns and understands the behaviors, attitudes, and skills that make up his or her new role. This socialization process includes both the formal orientation process that is structured and informal orientation that is provided by coworkers. When well done, these processes contribute to role clarity and help the employee see how he or she fits into the organization and contributes to its goals, all contributions toward employee engagement (Saks & Gruman, 2011). When they are ignored, or done badly, they begin a process of disillusionment and distrust.

In order to be effective in supporting employee engagement, the formal orientation process needs to provide new hires with the information that they need to feel valued; it needs to be predictable and orderly in order to promote a sense of psychological safety; and it needs to ensure that they can see that they will have the resources to be successful in the job. Employees who are clear about how they fit into an organization will generally see the experience as being meaningful and will feel more secure and therefore are more likely to be engaged. On the contrary, being left alone with little contact with others, not knowing time frames such as when probationary periods end, and not understanding how they will be evaluated all lead to a negative emotional state that is contrary to employee engagement (Saks & Gruman, 2011). As people change jobs more frequently than in the past, they experience new jobs more frequently, and the process of socialization becomes more important.

Performance Management and Rewards

Performance management is the sum of all of the policies and practices that interact to manage the work that is done by employees. According to researchers, less than one-third of employees believe that their organization's approach to managing their performance is effective (Gruman & Saks, 2011). Performance management systems affect levels of employee engagement through demonstrating organizational values and allowing employees to judge levels of organizational justice. Questions about whether supervisors understand accomplishments, whether their feedback reflects actual performance, or whether individuals understand what they need to do for a successful evaluation are all linked to the level of employee engagement. While the ultimate goal of performance management is enhanced performance, it also has other outcomes that affect employees' attitudes and connections with the organization. It is thus an important component of an environment that fosters employee engagement.

The appraisal component of performance management has a significant impact on employees' perceptions of fairness. Evaluations of items that are irrelevant or outside of the employee's control are perceived as violations of organizational justice and reduce the level of trust that the employee has in both the supervisor and the organization. Perceptions of fairness are supported by behavior that is predictable, consistent, clear, and nonthreatening and are increased when employees believe that their views are taken into account. Appraisals that incorporate sufficient notice, a fair hearing, and judgment based on evidence therefore increase employee engagement. An appraisal conversation is also a useful time to discuss levels of engagement with the employees and how they could be enhanced.

A colleague shared this story with me:

> My supervisor called me to her office to talk about a complaint that she had received from a customer. After she told me what the customer had said, I asked her if I could tell her my side of the story. She said no because we are expected to provide excellent service no matter what and therefore what I had to say "was not relevant." Although I was polite to her, inside I was thinking that if she wouldn't listen to me, there was really no reason why I should listen to her.

Traditional forms of performance evaluation were appropriate during times when jobs were stable with clear and easily observable procedures. As organizations find themselves in periods of rapid change such as that in the library and information environment, employers are looking for creativity, personal initiative, and adaptability in their employees. These are not easily measurable in the traditional way. Rather than looking at performance management, some organizations are beginning to look at performance facilitation, seeking ways to improve performance (Gruman & Saks, 2011). This is becoming more common in knowledge- and service-based industries, which share many characteristics with libraries and information services. Work in these environments is varied and subtle, changing the focus toward what gets accomplished and away from how the work gets done.

In general, performance management systems are variations of a model that includes setting performance goals, assessing progress toward goals, and providing feedback to employees about their progress. Depending on how these steps are enacted, they may have a positive or negative effect on employee engagement. Reshaping the ways in which they are used can support a high engagement climate. For example, requiring employee participation in the goal-setting stage so that employees perceive that there is a negotiation will enhance perceptions of control. This is a good opportunity for supervisors to discuss elements of the psychological contract with employees to discover whether goals are aligned with employee expectations and provide sufficient levels of challenge combined with a likelihood of success. It is also the time to discuss individual goals that are not being met with the organization and discuss alternatives. This goes beyond finding out what developmental needs the employee identifies and incorporates individual needs, goals, and desires. It is critical to talk about how the employee will contribute to the success of the organization. This requires a different mind-set for supervisors as they give up a level of control and become facilitators and shift their focus from organizational goals to the integration of individual and organizational goals. The incorporation of employee values and interests will contribute to a higher level of engagement. Success in achieving goals that are not important to an individual will not promote his or her sense of personal well-being or level of engagement (Gruman & Saks, 2011).

An individual's psychological contract is related to levels of engagement: to the extent that an employee expects his or her work to be meaningful and expects the employer to provide both material resources and support so that he or she can be successful. Performance facilitation processes support this by finding out what part of the work is meaningful to the employees and the extent to which they perceive appropriate levels of support. Managers often fail to take this into consideration during the performance management process and miss an opportunity to build engagement.

Coaching is an essential component of the performance management system and should not be limited to annual feedback during the appraisal process. Being available to assist employees when they are planning their work, providing support when difficulties arise, and recognizing achievements on a regular basis all help to foster engagement. These activities support a higher level of resilience among employees, which contributes to positive adjustment to change, and to being able to move on and recover from challenging situations. This leads to a higher level of employee confidence in their ability to be successful and increases the likelihood of engagement. This places a great deal of responsibility onto the supervisor, requiring skill at determining when an employee needs support or feedback and in understanding the work at a level that allows for the feedback to be meaningful.

The quality of the relationship between the supervisor and the employee is a significant component of performance management. Managers who are skilled at supporting employees make a significant contribution to engagement. Exhibiting transformational leadership skills to inspire and engage employees is critical, so this in an area that organizations must incorporate into supervisor training, expectations, and evaluation. Modern, nimble organizations make it difficult for supervisors to manage employee performance, so changing the approach so that supervisors manage the context of performance is likely to be more successful as well as increasing levels of employee engagement. Managers who ensure that expectations are congruent with individual goals, who provide the resources needed and support when required, who provide appropriate feedback, and who treat all employees with respect will have a positive impact on the levels of engagement.

Organizational Structure

Many organizations have silos within them, either as an explicit part of the structure or as an implicit understanding of how things work. They may be formalized through lines of authority and physical structures such as the location of departments and offices, or they may exist only within the minds of employees. Silos create boundaries, either physical or psychological, that inhibit collaboration between departments. Getting approval becomes time-consuming as requests for permission and other communications move to the top of one silo before making the jump to another one. In this way, silos limit autonomy (Diamond & Allcorn, 2009).

In a rapidly changing environment, organizational structures need to be flexible, with looser rules, in order to allow staff members to adapt to change. Many library and information organizations developed their structure during times of greater stability, and their procedures and decision-making processes reflect a greater level of rigidity. This prevents managers from introducing changes in the way in which they deal with employees and hampers their ability to be responsive to the environment. Cross-functional teams, for example, can introduce greater levels of flexibility as well as create opportunities for staff members to learn new skills and contribute unique perspectives.

The Role of Perception

Life would be very much easier if everyone understood what we intended when we said something. Unfortunately, that is not yet possible, so it is important to understand the role of perception when looking at management practices. In order for policies or practices to affect how employees behave, they need to be both recognized and interpreted by employees. Typically, when we assess our organizations, we look at descriptive measures, such as whether or not there is a performance management system in place, rather than trying to determine whether it is effective and its overall impact on the organization. The question of how employees perceive and interpret the system is almost never addressed. Some writers have argued that poor or uneven implementation of policy and practice is actually detrimental to an organization and has a more negative impact than if there were no policies (Shantz et al., 2016).

Specific Strategies for Addressing Engagement

While many organizations talk at a management level about engagement, they are not consistent about involving their employees in the discussion. In order to increase overall engagement levels, strategies must be something that are thought about, talked about, and acted upon. Engagement must be defined in terms that people understand and can identify with personally. For example, if boosting recognition is one of your engagement strategies, you could ask at a staff meeting what it would take for everyone to be able to say that they had received recognition for good work during the past two weeks (Knight, 2013). For this to be successful, managers must be able to listen and incorporate this feedback into their own behavior without being defensive. This does not mean that the feedback has to come from the manager; the staff members should also discuss how the feedback can be delivered and who can provide it, including coworkers and customers. These discussions may be led by employees, allowing them to develop their skills, and report back to the manager.

Is There a Downside to Engagement?

As employee engagement becomes popular in the management literature, and more organizations consider trying to increase engagement in order to boost productivity, it is useful to stop and consider whether it is possible to have too much of a good thing. Some of the considerations raised in the literature include rising levels of inequality at work with engaged employees working harder and longer, the legitimacy of organizations deliberately nurturing higher engagement levels but failing to recognize or reward them, and the potential for harm to a highly engaged worker's work-home balance (Truss, Shantz, Soane, Alfes, & Delbridge, 2013).

Employees who are highly engaged may lack energy to maintain their home life, having expended it all in their working life. Work may then start to interfere with their family commitments. High levels of engagement may also contribute to role overload, resulting in stress rather than reducing it. This has been demonstrated to vary by personality type, with more conscientious employees having better skills to manage their personal resources such as time and energy (Bolino, Klotz, Turnley, & Harvey, 2013). High levels of engagement at work can also lead to frustration or resentment when family commitments interfere with their work; this may be more frequent when these commitments break into the momentum that an employee has developed in engaging with their responsibilities.

It is also possible that being highly engaged becomes the norm in an organization, and any employees who are not highly engaged are perceived to be less than successful. In this way, they are under extreme pressure to either appear to be engaged or to do more in order to be seen to be meeting escalating expectations, either of which can contribute to stress and ultimately burnout. In this setting, just meeting the expectations of the job becomes insufficient (Bolino, Klotz, Turnley, & Harvey, 2013).

Another potential negative impact that affects both the employee and the organization is that employee engagement can become self-reinforcing. By focusing on behaviors that are rewarded, employees may neglect other less appealing parts of their job. In this way, they may redesign their jobs so that they are able to focus on the parts that they find engaging, which may not be in the organization's best interests (Halbesleben, 2011).

REFLECTION QUESTIONS

The questions below can be used for personal reflection or to stimulate discussion in staff groups.

1. Consider the mission statement or planning documents of your organization. Do they play a daily part in the lives of employees, for example, by being used as a reference point when setting expectations? There are several ways in which they can be integrated throughout the organization in terms of motivating employees and engaging them in the work of the organization. To what extent are employees aware of these framework documents? Consider ways in which they might be more useful.

2. When you look at the recruitment process for your organization, is it well aligned and integrated with the actual work that people are expected to do after they are hired? Is there any opportunity for you to influence this process so that it is more useful both in recruiting the people who are needed and providing them with the first step of orienting them to the climate and culture of your workplace?

6

Professional Associations, Library and Information Training Programs, and Unions

Part of the work environment that is tangential to the employing organization is the impact of training programs, professional associations, and unions or faculty associations. While the research linking these directly with employee engagement is scarce, and there is very little in the library and information literature, there are some connections that can be readily made from the other literature. These are part of the environment that library and information practitioners work within and help to shape their employment experience.

In particular, positive and effective relationships can be extended to include those formed through professional association activities or participation in union or faculty association activities. Perceptions of meaningful and worthwhile work are partially shaped by the original socialization that takes place during the education received during an individual's entry into the profession. Perceived organizational support can be shaped by union or faculty association contracts. These contracts also have a significant impact on levels of autonomy and can help to support role clarity by defining jobs. Finally, union or faculty association contracts are often the source of organizational policies and practices that underlie perceptions of organizational justice.

While these effects are interwoven, for the sake of clarity they are reviewed separately. A discussion of professional identity and professional commitment provides a framework for thinking about the impact that training, associations, and union or faculty association contracts have on employee engagement.

PROFESSIONAL IDENTITY AND PROFESSIONAL COMMITMENT

The terms *professional identity* and *professional commitment* are often used interchangeably, although they are somewhat different. Professional identity refers to how people identify themselves in the context of their work and the extent to which individuals identify themselves with their profession. It has three interacting components: the self-image, the occupational role, and the expectations of others. Professional identity is generally developed through interaction with others but is expressed individually as "who I am" or "who I want to be." Professional commitment, on the other hand, describes the extent to which individuals feel tied to their profession, so a strong professional identity is often combined with a strong professional commitment.

Professional identity has a significant impact on determining behavior at work, and those with a strong professional identity are less likely to leave the profession and more likely to undertake activities that benefit the profession. Professional commitment and professional identity have a strong connection with employee engagement, particularly when organizational goals and values are aligned with professional goals and values. Both professional identity and professional commitment interact with a positive work climate; the more supportive the climate, the more individuals feel connected with their profession as well as with their employer. Increasing levels of professional identity and professional commitment should be of interest to managers as they increase the relative importance of intrinsic values to extrinsic values (Caricati et al., 2014).

One of the factors of employee engagement is the level of dedication experienced by the engaged employees, which indicates the level of identification that they have with their job. In general, professional employees exhibit higher levels of engagement as a result of their connection with their profession. Individuals with strong professional identities have demonstrated that they are more highly committed to their organizations and their customers. As they are doing meaningful work that is aligned with their values, their professional commitment grows. The more engaged they are, the more they are absorbed in their work and the more they will choose to invest in their profession, increasing their level of professional commitment (Yalabik, van Rossenberg, Kinnie, & Swart, 2015).

Significant and positive relationships between selected activities and the support of professional commitment include reading professional journals and being involved in professional associations. Given the strong interaction between professional commitment and employee engagement, organizations should consider ways to support and encourage these behaviors through financial support and time or through recognition. In particular, these activities and the increased level of professional commitment help individuals to succeed during times of significant change as they support adaptation through professional development and redefining of professional roles.

In a study of Canadian librarians, professional identity was shown to have a positive correlation with employee engagement (Law, 2015). Professional identity forms through a socialization process that includes the initial professional training as well as socialization through professional associations and in the work environment. It includes observation of role models, the sharing of common expertise or values, and feedback on different behaviors. Professional identity includes both a cognitive component made up of skills, knowledge, and behavior and a psychological component made up of the values, attitudes, and goals of the profession. These are internalized in varying amounts to form the professional identity that aligns the individual with other members of the profession (Maclellan, Lordly, & Gingras, 2011).

An individual's professional identity helps to shape relationships with coworkers and with employers. It is particularly significant during periods of change such as that experienced in the library and information environment. There is also a particular link with autonomy as professional identity includes the values and beliefs that are used to support professional judgments.

Stereotype threat occurs when an individual fears confirming the stereotype about his or her identity, and it has a negative impact on emotions and behavior, resulting in increased stress and reduced performance in the workplace (Wheeler, 2014). It reduces career ambitions and reduces trust and the sense of belonging. It occurs regardless of any overt behavior. The occurrence of stereotype threat in the library community has not been studied, although there are a significant number of studies on the frequency of negative stereotypes in literature and in various media. Both library and information training programs and professional associations need to take steps to reduce the impact of a negative stereotype of librarians by providing role models who are able to demonstrate that the stereotype is untrue (Wheeler, 2014).

LIBRARY AND INFORMATION PROGRAMS

Library and information programs vary across the world: they may be a technical certificate, an undergraduate degree, or a graduate degree. Regardless of the specific program, they all serve as the entryway into the profession and practice of librarianship. As such, they play a major role in the socialization of library and information professionals, which, combined with the nature of the workplace, will have a long-term effect on their success. Engaged employees serve as examples to others and draw them into the occupation. Disengaged employees likewise discourage recruitment and serve as poor examples for students and new entrants into the field.

Traditionally, professional education in any field was focused on the competencies and skills needed to be successful after graduation. At the same time, sometimes inadvertently, students developed a sense of the values and beliefs that were part of a given profession. As the employment environment continues to change, graduates need not only new competencies but also new attitudes and a sense of their ability to fit into the organizations that will employ them. A new focus on the development of professional identity in professional education will bring some of these changes to the forefront. Professional socialization should be provided by a mix of practitioners and faculty who can be role models as well as significant exposure to experiential learning. Professional identity then becomes the mechanism for professionalization (Mylrea, Sen Gupta, & Glass, 2015). As well as the skills needed to start their new career, students develop the values and attitudes to drive their behavior and the specialized language of the profession. These values will include a commitment to lifelong self-improvement and service improvements through innovation and an orientation toward service and pride in their chosen profession. Socialization begins when students choose their course of study and continues throughout their career. The resulting professional identity, if positive, will lead to increased engagement, as it provides meaning to the work that they are doing.

In addition, library and information training programs can provide continuing professional development, often in a more formal way than professional associations, through the provision of certification. Formal professional development that enhances knowledge in a particular area provides greater professional standing as well as strengthens a positive professional identity. Greater skills provide greater opportunities for autonomy as well as increased professional pride, all of which contribute to a more positive professional identity and nurture employee engagement. Advanced professional development environments can also help to supply resources that may be missing in the workplace, such as support from like-minded colleagues and a level of intellectual challenge (Neary, 2014).

The scope and type of professional training programs have a significant effect on the process of developing a professional identity because it is the time and place in which students form a new identity for themselves as a member of the profession (Maclellan et al., 2011). This new identity has to live alongside their previous identities, and there may be areas of incongruence that have to be navigated. The newly forming professional identity is what will identify them as library and information practitioners and define how they are different from other professionals. It may also create conflict later as students may find that the idealized role that was developed during the training process is a poor match with the role in which they are employed. Students will also start to identify role models among practitioners with whom they interact. Faculty, at this point, have a significant role in socialization and development of professional identity and thus help to develop both the professional identity and the psychological contract of future employees.

Additionally, professional education is often the first introduction that the student has to management teaching. In order to support the potential engagement of future employees, it is important that students learn not only the processes of management but also how to develop and maintain a climate that recognizes individuals' need for autonomy and how to nurture trust. A study of the expectations of new library and information graduates showed that they assumed that they would be employed in a situation that allowed them to engage with their work with autonomy, supported by recognition and respect. Money was the least of their motivations as long as there was enough to support a reasonable quality of life (Singh, 2016).

This is not to suggest that library and information training programs are not changing and evolving, but the progress is inconsistent, partly due to the bureaucracy in academic institutions that hinders rapid change. Unfortunately, traditional competency training does not necessarily support the development of a professional identity that will interact successfully with the modern workplace. For example, a study of American librarians found that only 21% feel that their library education had prepared them for working with multiple cultures, although this has been identified as a need by employers (Adkins, Virden, & Yier, 2015). The authors conclude by reminding readers that professional responsibilities require librarians to change themselves and their practices, a function of professional identity.

Specific research shows the contribution that field experience plays in the development of professional identity. It may be called by other names but refers to the opportunity for students to have a period of practical learning experience. For it to make a useful contribution to the developing professional identity, field experience must allow students to engage in professional work that is supervised and evaluated and work alongside librarians rather than support staff (Hoffmann & Berg, 2014). Students report that field experience allows them to apply the theoretical learning from the classroom in an integrated way as well as learning about working conditions such as workload, committee work, and professional politics. A positive field experience allows students to develop a sense of belonging to the profession and the community of professionals and reduces "practice shock" after they graduate.

The development of professional identity among library and information students may become more of a challenge as programs evolve from the traditional classroom teaching model to online courses and other distance initiatives. It may be more difficult for students in online or distance programs to develop a sense of who they are as professionals and how they will engage with other professionals in the library and information environment. Suggestions from other fields such as teaching may provide options. For example, an online discussion forum involving both practitioners and students provides an opportunity for integrating theory and practice. It exposes students to different perspectives based in the complexity of practice (Sutherland & Markauskaite, 2012).

Professional training programs also contribute to the development of the psychological contract. Individuals beginning their first professional job will have ideas about what their employer will provide for them and what they will contribute to their employer. Many of these ideas are formed during the formal professional training period. When both employers and employees are able to satisfy the expectations of the psychological contract, there are opportunities for professional success and movement toward organizational goals (Dollansky, 2014). Field experience is particularly valuable in helping students to form realistic psychological contracts and develop an understanding of roles and expectations.

As individuals who develop professional training programs are considering the value of field experience, they should review the model of the realistic job preview. A realistic job preview is designed to communicate both the good and bad aspects of a job to a potential candidate. The purpose of a realistic job preview is to allow the candidate to determine for himself or herself whether or not the job is a good fit for his or her interests and values. As well as gaining experience during fieldwork, students should be encouraged to think critically about their needs and the likelihood that they will feel successful in the job.

If fieldwork is not a component of the training program, then students should be exposed to practitioners who are encouraged to speak freely about both the positive and negative sides of their jobs. Many students enter professional training with an idealized notion of what the actual job entails, and exposure to others' lived experience can help them to shape a more realistic psychological contract.

A colleague shared this story:

> This situation is sort of funny and sort of sad. We had a student from the local library school come and work with us for a month. It was her field experience, a part of her overall program. She seemed to fit in well, and was a diligent employee. During the exit interview, however, she revealed that she was really disappointed in the experience. When we probed a little, she shared that she had chosen to become a librarian because she wanted a job that was intellectual. To her dismay, during coffee breaks, instead of talking about great books, or great ideas, we chatted about day-to-day things, such as children, gardening, and the weather. I was never sure afterward how I felt about her decision to abandon librarianship and pursue an academic career.

Library and information training programs should also explore the idea of person-environment fit with students. This theory is based on the idea that every person and every environment have specific traits, and the closer the fit between the traits of the person and those of the environment, the higher the likelihood of a successful match. A good match will increase satisfaction, and a poor fit will increase stress. An understanding of personal needs, interests, and values and the values and rewards offered in a particular work environment are essential components of a good fit.

A good person-environment fit includes both objective and subjective measures. An objective measure could refer to something like salary; if you are a person who desires a high salary and the environment you are entering is not known for this, it is clear that this is not a good fit. A subjective measure refers to something less clear, for example, the need for autonomy. An honest appraisal of an individual's need for autonomy and an understanding of the freedom for decision making within a particular profession may lead to a more realistic understanding of the job ahead. This evaluation must recognize that both the individual and the employer have expectations, just as both have some ability to meet the expectations of the other (Edwards & Rothbard, 1999).

Specific skills can be introduced to smooth the transition from professional training to work and lessen the reality shock. These include self-management techniques (e.g., managing frustration, stress, and anxiety). Improved communication strategies include ways of questioning for clarity in order to maintain respectful relationships while still getting the information that is needed. New employees need the ability to demonstrate empathy and respect for others' perspectives while still contributing their skills and knowledge. These will be conducive to both a smooth transition and employee well-being (EWB).

EWB has a significant impact on many positive outcomes, including job satisfaction and employee engagement. A good person-environment fit, particularly when it focuses on values, is a contributor to EWB. As psychological breach has a significant negative impact on employee engagement, the role of the preliminary professional training in developing an appropriate psychological contract cannot be underestimated. Thus, both person-environment fit and the psychological contract are important for training programs to address in order to support the future success of their graduates.

PROFESSIONAL ASSOCIATIONS

Professional associations also have a significant role to play in the development and maintenance of professional identities and the enhancement of employee engagement. Their contribution to employee engagement is in several areas: exploring changes in professional identity, providing opportunities for networking and the discussion of common professional concerns, encouraging and supporting professional development, providing a source for peer support, and mentoring and acting as a voice for the profession (Darcy & Abed-Faghri, 2013).

Professional identity reflects an alignment of the individual's personal beliefs and values with that of other members of the profession. As the environment changes, these beliefs and values must shift to encompass new ways of thinking and acting. Professional associations provide a forum for exploring these changes and understanding them in the larger context of professional skills, outside of the limits of organizational goals. The norms of the profession contribute to professional identity and provide a sense of meaningfulness, one of the conditions that supports employee engagement (Popova-Nowak, n.d.).

For example, a review of the Medical Library Association's statement on research policy showed that the need for evidence-based research by its members had changed since the policy was originally written. The new policy, resulting from extensive consultation with members, included the statement that the association as well as its members would promote the expectation that all decision making in libraries would be evidence based and that library educators would include the skills that students need to be reflective practitioners as part of their professional preparation. These actions are part of a larger agreement about the value of a research culture (Grefsheim, Rankin, Perry, & McKibbon, 2008). The responsibility for moving this value into action is shared by the entire community of practice and thus becomes part of the professional identity of a medical librarian. Regardless of the support for research in an employer's organization, a medical librarian can find encouragement among a group of peers and develop skills in a supportive environment.

Professional associations provide opportunities for professional development to help members develop the knowledge and skills to adapt new technologies and to develop management skills or soft skills that are needed to be successful. Ongoing professional development supports individuals' perceptions that they have the knowledge that they need to be successful, increasing their competence and contributing to their level of engagement. As well as addressing current needs, it supports individuals' aspirations (Neary, 2014).

The networking potential provided by participation in professional associations provides an opportunity for the development of collaborative activities with like-minded colleagues and provides a platform for individuals who want to have a broader impact, for example, through the development of standards. It provides both a source and a sounding board for new ideas. Becoming a member of an association's executive committee can be a learning opportunity for developing experience in skills that are not currently part of an individual's job but are needed for promotion to leadership or management positions. For example, being the treasurer of an organization provides experience with budgets, fund management, and audits (Henson, 2016).

One of the other significant roles for professional associations is the need to present the profession to employers and to the public in a way that enhances the understanding of the value that the profession contributes to the community. This presentation needs to be articulated in a way that is meaningful both to people familiar with the profession, such as members and employers, and to decision makers who may have outdated or incorrect notions. There is a significant challenge in ensuring that the perception of the profession is stable enough to focus the public's attention but changes enough to include new skills and concerns in relation to a changing environment. This is a particular challenge in the current library and information environment as many movies and books support a perception of librarians that is out of date and does not include the value added to them in a technological information environment.

One of the threats to the professional identity of librarians that can be addressed by library associations results from increasing overlap with information technology professionals and the importance of generic skills, such as good communication skills, in recruitment and evaluation. In particular, in many countries, senior librarians such as library directors come with other qualifications from areas such as business or finance. In some university settings, faculty members from any discipline may be appointed as chief librarian. Since trust in senior management makes such a large contribution to employee engagement, the question of qualifications is one that must be addressed continually by professional associations (Wilson & Halpin, 2006).

The creation of meaning about the profession supports stronger professional identities by increasing self-esteem among the members, which has a strong correlation with employee engagement (Neary, 2014). This sense of shared meaning provides value to the members of the professional group; it is difficult to imagine how members of a profession can expect to be valued by others if they do not have a clear and shared feeling about their identity as a member of a profession and a positive belief about the value of that profession (MacLellan, Lordly & Gingras, 2011). Professional identity is the source of the information that the members of the profession project to others, including clients, other professionals, and decision makers.

Professional socialization is a career-long process that constantly reshapes and confirms professional identity. While professional programs in universities and colleges have a significant impact at the beginning of a career, the ongoing process is shaped by associations, workplaces, and other groups. Thus, professional associations support professional identities that reflect expertise as well as contributions to the profession through teaching, mentoring, and advocacy.

UNIONS AND FACULTY ASSOCIATIONS

The relationship between union/faculty association membership and employee engagement is underrepresented in the literature. However, to the extent that unions and faculty associations develop, implement, and monitor workplace processes, they clearly contribute to the perceptions of organizational justice. Their intentions to ensure consistent application of processes to all individuals over time, free from bias, support procedural justice. Their delineation of appeal processes ensure that individuals have the opportunity to question and contribute additional information and alternative explanations, which are also an essential part of organizational justice (Brown, Bemmels, & Barclay, 2010). Since union agreements are negotiated with management rather than being set by management, there is an opportunity for employees to contribute to the development of fair policies, as a separate component of justice, prior to their implementation. Believing that the policies are fair contributes to organizational citizenship behavior, even in instances where it is believed that the implementation of the policies has been unfair.

Unions play a role in providing employees with an opportunity to provide honest input and to challenge managerial authority. Management-sponsored participation in decision making may be perceived as having potential reprisals, particularly if the input is contrary to management preferences. This opportunity for independent input, and for independent assessment of the application of procedures, can contribute to employee engagement (Gill, 2009).

Unions also help to establish the psychological contract. Because the contract is written and monitored, individuals can look to it for information about how the organization should work. It provides information about the kind of treatment they can expect from a supervisor. Recent research into union membership and employee engagement in the United States found that although nonunionized employees were more satisfied with many elements of their work than unionized employees, their levels of engagement were similar (Modern Survey, 2015). The same study found that nonunionized employees were slightly more likely to contribute extra effort above and beyond their assigned responsibilities to support organizational goals. They also report somewhat more favorable impressions of their supervisors and significantly more favorable impressions of senior leadership.

While there are many studies that look at the impact of faculty status on librarians, the relationship between faculty status and employee engagement is yet to be investigated. Extrapolating from other research, however, suggests that faculty status for academic librarians can contribute to increased levels of employee engagement through supporting opportunities for participation in decision making and increasing levels of autonomy. The contracts signed by faculty associations on behalf of librarians contribute to a sense of organizational justice by providing a fair and equitable approach to many human resource practices and providing a voice for librarians to question decisions. Faculty associations strive to unpick the relationships of power that exist in hierarchical relationships, and these can provide opportunities for engagement (Shuck, Collins, Rocco, & Diaz, 2016).

REFLECTION QUESTIONS

The questions below can be used for personal reflection or to stimulate discussion in staff groups.

1. Remembering your early professional training and your entry into your current profession, do you think that you were prepared for the reality of the job? What misperceptions did you have about the kind of work you would be doing, the conditions of the job, or the values of the organization where you worked? Based on this, how could the training of new recruits into library and information be improved to lessen the shock they experience in the transition from education to the workplace?

2. Do you feel that participation in professional associations helps you to think about the issues related to your profession? If not, what is the benefit of membership in a professional association? Would you encourage younger colleagues to get involved in professional activities outside of the workplace, and if so, why? The answers to these questions may lead you to think about your relationship with professional colleagues.

7

Evaluation and Change

The level of employee engagement in an organization can be evaluated in many ways, both formal and informal. Additionally, there are ways to assess the nature of the conditions and climate that are antecedents of employee engagement. Like any other request for information from employees, it is necessary to listen to the responses. If employees perceive that asking for their opinion is an activity without results, and that management has no intention of taking any action, they are likely to stop providing useful feedback.

The illusion of providing opportunities for communication without doing anything about it is called "pseudo voice." It is common even in organizations that say that they are committed to employee input, particularly when managers are expected to ask for employee feedback even if they are uncomfortable with it or have no intention of following through. Pretending to be interested has more negative impact than not asking at all (Vries, Jehn, & Terwel, 2012). It reduces the level of trust in management with negative effects on employee engagement. Similarly, if employees believe that management only uses information from their input that is aligned with what management wants, they will come to distrust the feedback and communication process.

Employees may attribute pseudo voice to many things, for example, that the manager or supervisor prefers an autocratic style while the organization requires a more democratic style. Participation and open communication may be stated as part of an organization's values and climate, but these values may not be shared by all managers. Managers may then attempt to deceive employees, by saying that their opinions matter, in an attempt to create an illusion of fairness (Vries et al., 2012). This disconnect between articulated values and actual behavior will undermine employee engagement.

EVALUATING ENGAGEMENT

Formal measures of employee engagement are typically annual surveys and are subject to all of the same questions as other regular surveys. Assuming that employees trust the organization enough to provide honest answers, they can give management information at the group level of how employees perceive their own levels of engagement or of the conditions in the organizational climate that contribute to engagement. The information becomes dated quickly and provides a snapshot of what is in employees' minds the day they respond. There is also the potential for biased responses as employees report what they think management wants or expects to hear.

Specific steps should be followed to provide the best outcome from an employee survey. Before the survey is rolled out, there must be a planning stage to determine how the survey will be administered, who will deal with the responses, who will have access to the data and in which form, and how confidentiality is to be maintained. This must all be communicated to staff members with a general timeline and a period allowed for questions and concerns to be raised. The survey must be chosen or designed to provide information that can be translated into action. When the survey has been completed, the results should be shared with employees in a way that is clear and leads to a discussion about both what is done well and areas for attention or improvement. When an action plan has been developed, it needs to be communicated back to the employees and related to the survey results.

The management literature provides various evaluation methods for determining the level of employee engagement across an organization. These methods can be adapted for use in a particular unit or department, with the language amended to reflect the library and information environment. For example, Kumar and Pansari (2015) describe an employee engagement scorecard that can be easily modified. It provides feedback at a group level on issues that contribute to engagement, including the level of satisfaction with the organization's operations, identification with the organization, commitment to meeting the organization's goals, a sense of loyalty, and beliefs about performance.

The test of employee engagement that is most often used in research is that developed by Schaufeli (Schaufeli, Salanova, Gonzalez-Roma, & Bakker, 2002). It is a straightforward list of statements that employees are able to respond to. For example, "At my job I am very resilient mentally" provides insight into the level of energy that employees are able to bring to their work. "My job inspires me" allows an employee to think about how meaningful his or her current job is and whether it is aligned with his or her personal goals and aspirations. The response to the statement "I am immersed in my work" is an indicator of the level of absorption that employees are experiencing.

You have the option of developing your own survey based on the particular issues that you are concerned about in your workplace and using the research literature to help you formulate questions. Surveys are also available that can be purchased from different consulting companies.

Managers' engagement levels have a direct impact on employee engagement and have been estimated to account for up to 70% of the variance in levels of employee engagement (Gallup, Inc., 2015). For this reason, a manager who is interested in assessing the level of engagement in a workplace may wish to start by reflecting on his or her own level of engagement and how that is demonstrated and modeled for others. Managers, like all employees, need the resources and support necessary to learn and grow and need to feel competent and successful in order to feel engaged.

Some assessment of levels of engagement can be discovered by observation. For example, what can you tell about the level of discretionary work that is done by employees such as volunteering to organize events for coworkers? Can you observe examples of coworker support such as sharing information or offering to help colleagues who are struggling? A high absentee rate for small illnesses can also be an indicator of stress or disengagement.

Discussing employee engagement can be part of other conversations that managers have with employees and can be particularly useful during evaluation processes and when negotiating expectations. Ensuring that every employee understands how their work contributes to the organization's goals contributes to making their work meaningful, a critical driver of engagement. Does each employee feel that they are working with coworkers in a way that supports everyone, and are they able to learn from each other? This question often highlights a misalignment between rhetoric and practice in organizations that say they value teamwork but only reward individuals. Can they describe ways in which their competencies contribute to the success of the team? If not, there is a gap in the meaningfulness of their work experience. Do employees believe that they have the resources necessary to be successful in reaching their expectations? This may indicate that there is a barrier that prevents them from getting the resources or support that they need.

ASSESSING THE ORGANIZATIONAL CLIMATE

Employee engagement is highly correlated with perceptions of organizational climate, and some writers have suggested that a measure of employee engagement provides an estimate of climate perceptions (Gray, 2007, p. 23). It is quite difficult to assess your own organizational climate; since you work in it every day it becomes familiar and almost invisible. Nonetheless, a systematic effort to assess the climate provides information that can lead to improvements and increase the level of employee engagement.

The factors to consider when evaluating your organizational climate include the freedom to express opinions and to question decisions of others, a level of intrinsic satisfaction from meaningful work, and the opportunity to try new ideas. These are all positive factors and linked with autonomy, responsibility, and control. In general, people will be more engaged when they evaluate their organizational climate positively on these factors (Gray, 2007).

In a positive climate, new ideas are listened to and considered, and there are the minimum number of rules that are required for smooth operations. The freedom to speak out knowing that your ideas will be heard contributes to a sense of genuine participation in defining goals and expectations. There is a level of autonomy so that employees are able to work toward achieving their expectations without anyone looking over their shoulder or requiring constant approval. This requires that managers are skilled at delegation, including holding employees responsible for success. This leads to the level of autonomy necessary for employees to exercise control over their own work and take pride in it when it is completed. Clarity contributes to a positive organizational climate. People need to understand expectations and be clear about what their work contributes to the achievement of organizational goals. Clarity includes setting standards for evaluation and applying them fairly.

As with other workplace assessments, it is important to be clear with employees why you are asking questions and what you plan to do with their input. Collecting it and ignoring it will provide negative outcomes, including distrust and cynicism. The information can be asked as part of a survey or through other methods like interviews. Each organization must weigh the value of anonymous responses against the kinds of in-depth conversations that can be held face-to-face.

Managers can also take steps to begin to assess the workplace climate through taking a close look at the organization. This review can take place organization-wide or within a particular unit or department. Some of the questions to be considered include the following:

- How do we get our work done? Are we collaborative, or do we expect people to work independently? If it is a combination of ways, how do we decide which way we will use and how do the people involved know? Does our appraisal system reward the kind of work that we say it does?

- Are we driven by consensus, or is there a level of authoritative decision making? Is this consistent throughout the organization?

- What is our preferred method of internal communication? Does information flow freely both upward and downward in the organization? Are there bottlenecks created by individuals or positions?

- What kinds of people are successful in this organization? Do we reward individual stars or team achievements? Is our assessment and reward structure clear, and do staff members perceive it to be fair?

- Is our structure hierarchical or flat, and how clear are the reporting and decision-making structures? Is there a way for new ideas to be considered at the appropriate level in the organization?

- Do our managers and staff have the resources they need to be successful? This includes consideration of workload, flexibility of schedules, and time. Do our managers have the skills to work with staff in a way that is aligned with organizational values?

The next, and harder step, is to determine whether the answers to these questions are the same when provided by managers and by employees. Regardless of what managers believe, employees make decisions based on their perceptions of the climate. For this reason, management must search for evidence that there is internal alignment between all of the structures that make up the climate, including policies, expectations, and behavior.

For example, an organization should not state that it has a climate that encourages teamwork if the processes and behavior reward and support competition and individual success. Participation and empowerment must be aligned with processes that allow individuals to make decisions about their own work and an understanding by both managers and employees that managers are not in charge of everything. A climate of openness needs to be aligned with behavior that allows individuals to bring forward their knowledge and ideas, even if they are unconventional or disagree with prevailing management beliefs. Performance appraisal systems that tie reward to merit often fail not because the standards are not fair, but because of a lack of openness and trust between individuals and their supervisors (Mozenter & Stickell, 2009).

Assessments often reveal areas of disagreement among managers or between management and employees. How these are treated by management will also reveal a great deal about the organization. Attempting to correct wrong perceptions that are held by staff members reveals that management has not taken the disconnect seriously and listened to what people had to say. Encouraging discussion about these perceptions can provide useful information for everyone in the organization. An article about an unsuccessful attempt to make changes in the merit system at an academic library summarized this by talking about what they learned through the communication process (Mozenter & Stickell, 2009). They refer to the dialogue on broader issues that concerned relationships among specific groups of staff members that had been beneath the surface for some time but became part of a formal discussion during the change process.

ASSESSING PERCEPTIONS OF ORGANIZATIONAL JUSTICE

Since organizational justice is a significant factor contributing to employee engagement, organizations may wish to assess employee perceptions of fairness. As with other assessments, this can be done in a variety of ways: by observation, by discussion, or by formal survey. When employees provide feedback, there is the same need to be seen to take action in response as there is with any other information provided by employees.

For determining the questions to ask, Colquitt's work on assessing organizational justice can provide many suggestions as well as showing one measure that is frequently used in research (Colquitt, 2001). For example, in assessing procedural justice, employees are asked whether procedures were based on accurate information. This is an essential component of performance appraisals, where employees need to believe that their supervisors have all of the information that they need to evaluate work. In assessing distributive justice, one of the questions asks whether an employee believes that the outcome of a decision reflects his or her contribution to the organization. Interpersonal justice is assessed by questions about whether an individual believes that he or she has been treated with dignity and respect. The measure of information justice includes questions about whether an employee perceives that he or she receives enough information and whether his or her supervisor is candid.

While many organizations have processes that are built on the concepts of justice, few assess whether their employees perceive these to be fair. By evaluating these perceptions, the organization can get some insight into how the organization's climate is experienced by employees, with some direction toward how it can be improved.

MAKING A CHANGE

A supportive organizational climate is linked to many positive outcomes for both the organization and the individual. There are many reasons, therefore, for every supervisor and manager to try to improve the climate of their workplace. Regardless of whether the motivation is for the good of the organization, or for the moral imperative of trying to improve the lives of coworkers, small changes can reap significant rewards. Managers and supervisors may not be able to change the entire organization, but they can change the part they have responsibility for.

Making changes in your organization's climate can be as stressful as any other kind of organizational change. It can provide opportunities for improvement and for both managers and employees to learn and grow. It also increases demands on everyone in the organization and will affect the organizational environment. Change is often accompanied by a sense of reduced control and lack of role clarity. As shifts occur, relationships among people change, including those which have been relied upon for social support. This all adds up to increased levels of stress.

Evidence shows, however, that a well-managed and healthy change process can go a long way to mitigate these negative conditions (Tvedt, Saksvik, & Nytrø, 2009). As well as the content of the change, the process, including planning, implementing, and evaluating, is critical to success. The beliefs of employees about their participation in the process as well as the context of the change will have a significant impact on the success of the change. One of the considerations when designing a healthy change process is awareness of the diversity of experiences. Throughout the change it is necessary to listen carefully for different reactions and ensure there is an open environment where employees feel free to speak about their reactions.

During any change process, the availability of managers to provide individualized information and respond to employee concerns provides a major support for success. This may also be a difficult time for managers who are, themselves, trying to understand and live within a new framework. Managers sometimes withdraw because they feel overwhelmed by the emotional responses of employees or because they feel unable to answer questions. Their availability, however, goes a long way in reducing uncertainty and confirms the positive intent and purpose of the change. This requires that managers not only have sufficient information but also understand and implement their roles in communication (Tvedt et al., 2009).

Throughout the change process, it is useful to accept resistance as a natural response to change, even when the purpose of the change is to improve the work environment. It is a rational response for a person who is facing ambiguity or unpredictability. If managers treat all responses seriously, regardless of whether they are about the content of the change or the process, employees will perceive that they are actually participants in the process rather than victims of it. Thus, dealing actively and constructively with resistance becomes part of the manager's communication role, and for the success of the change, this is a skill that managers require. An individual manager's position during change will be perceived to represent the organization as a whole and to symbolize whether or not the organization actually cares about employees' opinions. Extra attention paid to role clarification throughout the process will also contribute to a more successful change process. It reduces stress by helping employees understand their roles throughout the change process and their anticipated roles after the change is complete (Tvedt et al., 2009).

It is interesting to note that the conditions of a healthy change process are aligned with the conditions that contribute to employee engagement and also to a healthy workplace climate. The role of the direct supervisor or manager is critical in all of these situations, and therefore, organizations need to review the skills, knowledge, and attributes of all managers. It is essential that they are able to positively and successfully represent the organization to its employees. Managers' expectations and their evaluation and rewards must incorporate these factors if the organization is to be successful in making change.

CHANGE CAN BE MADE BY AN INDIVIDUAL

Many managers become frustrated because they feel that it is too difficult to change the way in which their organization deals with employees. While some organizational adjustments might be helpful to improve the organizational climate and nurture engagement, there are many changes that can be made by an individual manager or supervisor. The most significant indicator of organizational climate that is experienced by employees is the day-to-day behavior of their direct manager. The leadership style and actions of the manager have been estimated to account for more than half of organizational climate (Gray, 2007).

Managers have an obligation to foster a positive organizational climate, regardless of the effect on productivity, because of the positive impact on employee health and well-being. While they might not be able to change the entire organization, it is always possible to bring about changes by altering their own behavior. Changing behavior is not simple; it requires constant monitoring to avoid sliding back into old ways, particularly in times of stress. Fortunately, many of the changes that are required are relatively minor.

Change begins with self-knowledge. It can be very difficult to assess the climate of an organization where you have been for some time, because of the human tendency to adapt to gradual changes, even if they are negative. It is often the cumulation of small changes that leads to problems with organizational climate rather than a big or sudden shift.

Making a change in one's own behavior is not simple, even though it sounds like it should be. It is a long process that requires not only self-knowledge but also commitment and willpower. Support and recognition from the organization will help to cement new behaviors. Old habits are hard to shed. A prerequisite for that kind of change is the understanding that things could be better than they are now and a clear assessment of where things stand now.

Simple observation is a logical starting point. Observe your own interactions with coworkers, and try to determine whether they ever tell you bad news or criticize decisions that you make. If not, you might wonder if they actually feel as free to come and talk to you as you believe they are. If people do not perceive that they can speak to you freely, it does not really matter what you think.

A staff survey is another to gather information about staff perceptions of the organization. This can be adapted from one that is readily available or developed in-house. However, an important point to consider before you gather information is the obligation to act on the information you receive. The act of asking raises assumptions that something is going to change, and if there is no reaction, employees tend to become disillusioned. It is important to remember that this is about perceptions, and not "reality", and that the perceptions that are reported by staff may not be shared by managers.

A colleague shared this story:

> My manager says her door is always open, and I think she truly believes this.
> However, it is difficult to share information with her because she doesn't

actually listen to what you are trying to say. I went to tell her that several of my colleagues were concerned about safety issues during the late shift, but as soon as I started I felt like she was interrogating me, wanting to know who said what, and detailed questions about what happened and why we hadn't reported it. It resulted in a memo to my colleagues reminding us to report all incidents, and she actually hadn't heard what I was trying to say.

It can be very difficult to hear negative things about your management style when you survey staff, but it is the beginning of learning and positive change. When an employee expresses a concern, rather than interpreting it as a personal criticism, it can be viewed as input into improving the organization. Providing both formal and information channels for employee feedback becomes an invaluable source of information for organizational improvement, but only if the channels are perceived as being safe and comments are treated seriously. A willingness to listen and respond is the most effective way of encouraging employee input, but it needs to be seen as being both consistent and sincere.

Research suggests that only a small proportion of employees feel able to question their managers without being treated as though they were disloyal or lacked commitment to the organization. Questioning can serve two purposes, both useful to the organization. It can clarify expectations so that people understand how their work contributes to organizational goals. It can also offer new perspectives on decisions, which can lead to a more successful outcome. If managers are able to encourage staff members to question their decisions, their decision making should improve. This has the added benefit of more positive perceptions of organizational climate as a result of employees feeling that their input is valued.

YOU ARE THE ORGANIZATION

It is easy to feel that your organization is too big to change or is not willing to change. That does not mean that you are also unable to change. Employees judge their employers by their supervisors or managers and judge the entire organization based on their personal interactions. Therefore, any manager can improve perceptions of an organization by improving his or her interactions with employees. Interpersonal climate has a direct impact on employee behavior, so any manager can make an improvement.

Psychological safety, an atmosphere where employees feel secure, contributes to employee engagement. Feeling secure allows employees to show their true selves without fear of negative consequences. The main source of psychological safety is the supervisor. Supervisors are critical in creating an environment where employees feel encouraged to express their ideas. A supervisor who is inclusive demonstrates that the contributions of colleagues and staff members are welcomed and appreciated, even when they are questioning or disagreeing. This is perceived by employees as a sign that they are accepted and valued as part of the organization. Supervisor behavior is also used to judge how trustworthy the organization is. Encouraging staff members to contribute to shared goals, using facts to make decisions, and supporting collaboration will increase psychological safety as well as modeling desired behavior. In addition, staff members will watch to determine the extent to which supervisors' actions align with their words.

Integrity is demonstrated through honesty, consistency, and credibility in all situations. Supervisors must be careful not to make commitments that they cannot keep, as it is crucial that they provide models for employees regarding trustworthiness. They also model the kind of behavior that is expected in terms of complying with policies and procedures and embodying organizational values. Employees will judge the organization by whether supervisors work as hard as they do or feel that they are judged by a different set of standards. Good supervisors do not let their position fool them into thinking that they are always right. They demonstrate this by not assuming that they know more than the people doing the work and ask people to do things rather than demanding. As part of this, they take responsibility when things go wrong rather than trying to shift it onto other employees.

Communication with employees is a major factor in how supervisors are judged and how organizations are judged. Employees who feel that communication with their supervisor is frequent and open are more likely to develop good working relationships that underpin a higher level of organizational identification. This leads to greater productivity as well as better skills at dealing with organizational change and other stressful events at work. Communication is an area where even the most skilled supervisors can improve their skills.

If each supervisor in an organization improves his or her relationship with employees, gradually the entire organizational climate will change. In the short term, relationships will be improved, and, over time, employees' perceptions of the organization as a whole will improve leading to higher levels of engagement.

Following are the conditions that nurture employee engagement, detailed earlier in the book:

1. Positive and effective relationships with managers and coworkers and supervisor support
2. Interesting, worthwhile, and meaningful work
3. Sufficient resources to complete work successfully
4. Perceived organizational support
5. Autonomy
6. Role clarity
7. Organizational justice

Many of these are influenced by an individual supervisor, and each of them that is improved will have a positive effect on the organizational climate and on employee engagement.

Positive and effective relationships must be modeled by every supervisor and every manager. How they treat employees will be reflected both in how employees treat each other and how they treat customers. Paying attention to how you treat the people around you and improving your interpersonal skills result in an overall change in working conditions. Being a good listener and allowing staff members to express both new ideas and concerns improve the climate. Problems that are not expressed do not go away; they just hide until they turn into major issues. Humility as a manager can be expressed by being able to admit that you might be wrong and demonstrating this by responding to concerns about decisions. Good relationships are the foundation of perceived organizational support.

Interesting and worthwhile work may be limited by the organization and by job descriptions and contractual agreements. Within these boundaries, however, each supervisor can ensure that employees get the maximum amount of autonomy with as much variation as possible and desired by an individual employee. Questioning is one of the ways in which employees can check that they are doing the right thing. In some cultures, questioning is interpreted as disloyalty, and managers need to see it in a different light, as an indicator of lack of information or poor communication.

Sufficient resources to complete work may be out of any single manager's control, but there is an obligation for managers to do what they can to ensure that workloads are appropriate and that employees have sufficient time and skill to meet obligations. This often involves being an advocate for one's department with senior management. Staff members can support this advocacy by providing managers with data to make the case for additional resources.

Role clarity can always be improved by a supervisor. Outside of the formal job description, make sure that all staff members understand their job in terms of the value that they add for customers. Even cleaners have a role in satisfying customers by providing a clean and attractive facility. Ensure that each staff member knows and understands the criteria that are used in the assessment of their work. Each employee should understand where his or her job fits into the overall organizational structure and how it is interdependent with other jobs. These things should be explained to each new employee during orientation and reiterated annually as part of an appraisal process. Additionally, during any organizational change, each of these pieces of information needs to be revisited and articulated clearly.

Finally, organizational justice is demonstrated by each supervisor and assessed by each employee every time a decision is made. Consider the different forms of justice, and how a manager's perception of fairness may differ from that of an employee. Being able to articulate the process that is used to make a decision, the criteria that were used, and presenting the information in a respectful way will increase perceptions of organizational justice.

Each of the strategies suggested will make small changes in the right direction for improving organizational climate and increasing employee engagement. Every change will have an impact on other factors as well as on other people. As these changes accumulate, the organization will also change, as each employee is a component of the organization.

Working in an organization with a healthy climate is beneficial to everyone regardless of their role. It is engaging and satisfying. People want to work there and to do their best. This is a possibility for every organization as long as the people involved are willing to make the small changes that will accumulate and lead to a better workplace.

References

Abu-Shamaa, R., Al-Rabayah, W., & Khasawneh,T. (2015). The effect of job satisfaction and work engagement on organizational commitment. *IUP Journal of Organizational Behavior, 15*(4), 7–27.

Adkins, D., Virden, C., & Yier, C. (2015). Learning about diversity: The roles of LIS education, LIS associations, and lived experience. *Library Quarterly, 85*(2), 139–149.

Afacan Findikli, M. M. (2015). Exploring the consequences of work engagement: Relations among OCB-I, LMX and team work performance. *Ege Academic Review, 15*(2), 229–238.

Ahmed, I., Nawaz, M. M., Ali, G., & Islam, T. (2015). Perceived organizational support and its outcomes. *Management Research Review, 38*(7), 627–639.

Alfes, K., Truss, C., Soane, E. C., Rees, C., & Gatenby, M. (2013). The relationship between line manager behavior, perceived HRM practices, and individual performance: Examining the mediating role of engagement. *Human Resource Management, 52*(6), 839–859.

Barrick, M. R., Mount, M. K., & Li, N. (2013). The theory of purposeful work behavior: The role of personality, higher-order goals, and job characteristics. *Academy of Management Review, 38*(1), 132–153.

Barsoux, J., & Manzoni, J. F. (1998). *Procedural justice in action: Restructuring at Air France.* France: Fontainebleau.

Battistelli, A., Galletta, M., Portoghese, I., & Vandenberghe, C. (2013). Mindsets of commitment and motivation: Interrelationships and contribution to work outcomes. *Journal of Psychology, 147*(1), 17–48.

Bendassolli, P. F., Borges-Andrade, J., Alves, J. S. C., & de Lucena Torres, T. (2015). Meaningful work scale in creative industries: A confirmatory factor analysis. *Psico-USF, 20*(1), 1–12.

Biggio, G., & Cortese, C. G. (2013). Well-being in the workplace through interaction between individual characteristics and organizational context. *International Journal of Qualitative Studies on Health & Well-Being, 8*, 1–13.

Bingham, W. V. (1931). Management's concern with research in industrial psychology. *Harvard Business Review, 10*(1), 40.

Bolino, M. C., Klotz, A. C., Turnley, W. H., & Harvey, J. (2013). Exploring the dark side of organizational citizenship behavior. *Journal of Organizational Behavior*, 34(4), 542–559.

Breevaart, K., Bakker, A., Hetland, J., Demerouti, E., Olsen, O., & Espevik, R. (2014). Daily transactional and transformational leadership and daily employee engagement. *Journal of Occupational and Organizational Psychology*, 87(1), 138–157.

Brown, G., Bemmels, B., & Barclay, L. J. (2010). The importance of policy in perceptions of organizational justice. *Human Relations*, 63(10), 1587–1609.

Brunetto, Y., Shacklock, K., Teo, S., & Farr-Wharton, R. (2014). The impact of management on the engagement and well-being of high emotional labour employees. *International Journal of Human Resource Management*, 25(17), 2345.

Caesens, G., & Stinglhamber, F. (2014). Original article: The relationship between perceived organizational support and work engagement: The role of self-efficacy and its outcomes. *Revue Europeenne De Psychologie Appliquee*, 64, 259–267.

Caricati, L., Sala, R. L., Marletta, G., Pelosi, G., Ampollini, M., Fabbri, A., … Mancini, T. (2014). Work climate, work values and professional commitment as predictors of job satisfaction in nurses. *Journal of Nursing Management*, 22(8), 984–994.

Carr, J. Z., Schmidt, A. M., Ford, J. K., & DeShon, R. P. (2003). Climate perceptions matter: A meta-analytic path analysis relating molar climate, cognitive and affective states, and individual level work outcomes. *Journal of Applied Psychology*, 88(4), 605–619.

Carter, M. R., & Tourangeau, A. E. (2012, July). Staying in nursing: What factors determine whether nurses intend to remain employed? *Journal of Advanced Nursing*, 68(7), 1589–1600.

Chang, C., & Wu, C. (2013). Multilevel analysis of work context and social support climate in libraries. *Aslib Proceedings*, 65(6), 644.

Chaudhary, R., Rangnekar, S., & Barua, M. K. (2011). HRD climate and occupational self-efficacy as predictors of employee engagement. *Review of Management*, 1(3), 16–28.

Chen, C., Hsieh, C., & Chen, D. (2014). Fostering public service motivation through workplace trust: Evidence from public managers in Taiwan. *Public Administration*, 92(4), 954–973.

Cheng, Z. (2014). The effects of employee involvement and participation on subjective wellbeing: Evidence from urban China. *Social Indicators Research*, 118(2), 457–483.

Chiller, P., & Crisp, B. R. (2012). Professional supervision: A workforce retention strategy for social work? *Australian Social Work*, 65(2), 232–242.

Christian, L. A. (2015). A passion deficit: Occupational burnout and the new librarian. A recommendation report. *Southeastern Librarian*, 62(4), 2–11.

Colquitt, J. A. (2001). On the dimensionality of organizational justice: A construct validation of a measure. *Journal of Applied Psychology*, 86(3), 386–400.

Conrad, D. (2014). Workplace communication problems: Inquiries by employees and applicable solutions. *Journal of Business Studies Quarterly*, 5(4), 105–116.

Cooper, C. D., & Scandura, T. A. (2015). Getting to "Fair." *Journal of Leadership & Organizational Studies, 22*(4), 418–432. doi:10.1177/1548051815605021

The Corporate Agenda: Fiscal benefits of employee engagement. (2010, July). *Corporate Adviser,* 13.

Cropanzano, R., Bowen, D. E., & Gilliland, S. W. (2007). The management of organizational justice. *Academy of Management Perspectives, 21*(4), 34–48.

Danna, K., & Griffin, R. W. (1999). Health and well-being in the workplace: A review and synthesis of the literature. *Journal of Management, 25,* 357–384.

Darcy, M. G., & Abed-Faghri, N. (2013). The relationship between counselors and their state professional association: Exploring counselor professional identity. *Professional Counselor, 3*(3), 152–160.

Dekas, K. H., Bauer, T. N., Welle, B., Kurkoski, J., & Sullivan, S. (2013). Organizational citizenship behavior, version 2.0: A review and qualitative investigation of OCBs for knowledge workers at Google and beyond. *Academy of Management Perspectives, 27*(3), 219–237.

Desmidt, S. (2016). The relevance of mission statements: Analysing the antecedents of perceived message quality and its relationship to employee mission engagement. *Public Management Review, 18*(6), 894–917.

De Spiegelaere, S., Van Gyes, G., De Witte, H., & Van Hootegem, G. (2015). Job design, work engagement and innovative work behavior: A multi-level study on Karasek's learning hypothesis. *Management Revue, 26*(2), 123–137.

De Villiers, J. R., & Stander, M. W. (2011). Psychological empowerment, work engagement and turnover intention: The role of leader relations and role clarity in a financial institution. *Journal of Psychology in Africa, 21*(3), 405–412.

Diamond, M. A., & Allcorn, S. (2009). *Private selves in public organizations: The psychodynamics of organizational diagnosis and change.* New York, NY: Palgrave MacMillan.

Dollansky, T. D. (2014). The importance of the beginning teachers' psychological contract: A pathway toward flourishing in schools. *International Journal of Leadership in Education, 17*(4), 442–461.

Edwards, J. R., & Rothbard, N. P. (1999). Work and family stress and well-being: An examination of person-environment fit in the work and family domains. *Organizational Behavior and Human Decision Processes, 77*(2), 85–129.

Edwards, R. G., & Williams, C. J. (1998). Performance appraisal in academic libraries: Minor changes or major renovation? *Library Review, 47*(1–2), 14–19.

Freedman, S. (2014). Faculty status, tenure, and professional identity: A pilot study of academic librarians in New England. *Portal: Libraries and the Academy, 14*(4), 533–566.

Freeney, Y., & Fellenz, M. R. (2013). Work engagement, job design and the role of the social context at work: Exploring antecedents from a relational perspective. *Human Relations, 66*(11), 1427–1445.

Galagan, P. (2015). Employee engagement: An epic failure? *TD: Talent Development, 69*(3), 24.

Galbraith, Q., Fry, L., & Garrison, M. (2016). The impact of faculty status and gender on employee well-being in academic libraries. *College & Research Libraries, 77*(1), 71–86.

Gallup, Inc. (2015). *State of the American managers: Analytics and advice for leaders*. Retrieved August 16, 2016, from http://www.gallup.com/services/182138/state-american-manager.aspx

Ghosh, P., Rai, A., & Sinha, A. (2014). Organizational justice and employee engagement: Exploring the linkage in public sector banks in India. *Personnel Review*, 43(4), 628–652.

Gill, C. (2009). How unions impact on the state of the psychological contract to facilitate the adoption of new work practices (NWP). *New Zealand Journal of Employment Relations*, 34(2), 29–43.

Gillet, N., Colombat, P., Michinov, E., Pronost, A., & Fouquereau, E. (2013). Procedural justice, supervisor autonomy support, work satisfaction, organizational identification and job performance: The mediating role of need satisfaction and perceived organizational support. *Journal of Advanced Nursing*, 69(11), 2560–2571, 12 p. doi:10.1111/jan.12144

González-Romá, V., Schaufeli, W. B., Bakker, A. B., & Lloret, S. (2006). Burnout and work engagement: Independent factors or opposite poles? *Journal of Vocational Behavior*, 68, 165–174.

Gray, R. (2007). *A climate of success: Creating the right organizational climate for high performance*. Amsterdam, the Netherlands: Butterworth-Heinemann.

Grefsheim, S. F., Rankin, J. A., Perry, G. J., & McKibbon, K. A. (2008). Affirming our commitment to research: The medical library association's research policy statement: The process and findings. *Journal of the Medical Library Association*, 96(2), 114–120.

Gruman, J. A., & Saks, A. M. (2011). Performance management and employee engagement. *Human Resource Management Review*, 21, 123–136.

Gupta, V., & Kumar, S. (2013). Impact of performance appraisal justice on employee engagement: A study of Indian professionals. *Employee Relations*, 35(1), 61–78.

Halbesleben, J. R. B. (2011). The consequences of engagement: The good, the bad, and the ugly. *European Journal of Work & Organizational Psychology*, 20(1), 68.

Halbesleben, J. R. B., & Wheeler, A. R. (2015). To invest or not? The role of coworker support and trust in daily reciprocal gain spirals of helping behavior. *Journal of Management*, 41(6), 1628.

Hansen, A., Byrne, Z., & Kiersch, C. (2014). How interpersonal leadership relates to employee engagement. *Journal of Managerial Psychology*, 29(8), 953–972.

Harju, L. K., & Hakanen, J. J. (2016). An employee who was not there: A study of job boredom in white-collar work. *Personnel Review*, 45(2), 374–391.

Harwell, K. (2008). Burnout strategies for librarians. *Journal of Business & Finance Librarianship*, 13(3), 379–390.

He, H., Zhu, W. & Zheng, X. (2014). Procedural justice and employee engagement: Roles of organizational identification and moral identity centrality. *Journal of Business Ethics*, 122(4), 681–695.

Hellriegel, D., & Slocum, J. W. (1974). Organizational climate: Measures, research and contingencies. *Academy of Management Journal*, 17(2), 255–280.

Henson, J. W. (2016). Developing physician leaders through professional associations. *Journal of Healthcare Management*, 61(1), 7–10.

Herring, M. Y., & Gorman, M. (2003). Conference call: Do librarians with tenure get more respect? *American Libraries, 34*(6), 70–72.

Hoffmann, K., & Berg, S. (2014). "You can't learn it in school": Field experiences and their contributions to education and professional identity. *Canadian Journal of Information & Library Sciences, 38*(3), 220–238.

Hosel, H. V. (1984). Academic librarians and faculty status. *Journal of Library Administration, 5*(3), 57–66.

Hsiung, H., & Tsai, W. (2009). Job definition discrepancy between supervisors and subordinates: The antecedent role of LMX and outcomes. *Journal of Occupational & Organizational Psychology, 82*(1), 89–112.

Ilies, R., Aw, S. S. Y., & Pluut, H. (2015). Intraindividual models of employee well-being: What have we learned and where do we go from here? *European Journal of Work and Organizational Psychology, 24*(6), 827.

Jenkins, S., & Delbridge, R. (2013). Context matters: Examining "soft" and "hard" approaches to employee engagement in two workplaces. *International Journal of Human Resource Management, 24*(14), 2670.

Jones, S. J., & Taylor, C. M. (2012). Effects of institutional climate and culture on the perceptions of the working environments of public community colleges. *NASPA Journal about Women in Higher Education, 5*(1), 1–21.

Knight, M. (2013). Three strategies for making employee engagement stick. *Gallup Business Journal*, 1.

Kralj, A. L., & Solnet, D. J. (2011). *The influence of perceived organizational support on engagement: A cross-generational investigation in the hospitality industry*. Retrieved July 28, 2011, from http://scholarworks.umass.edu/cgi/viewcontent.cgi?article=1811&context=refereed

Kumar, V., & Pansari, A. (2015). Measuring the benefits of employee engagement. *MIT Sloan Management Review, 56*(4), 67–72.

Law, M. (2015). *Employee disengagement: The impact of role discrepancy, professional identity and organizational justice* (Doctoral dissertation, DTheses Athabasca University). doi:http://hdl.handle.net/10791/124

Lloyd, K., Boer, D., Keller, J., & Voelpel, S. (2015). Is my boss really listening to me? The impact of perceived supervisor listening on emotional exhaustion, turnover intention, and organizational citizenship behavior. *Journal of Business Ethics, 130*(3), 509–524.

Lynch, B. P., & Smith, K. R. (2001). The changing nature of work in academic libraries. *College & Research Libraries, 62*(5), 407–420.

Macey, W. H., & Schneider, B. (2008). The meaning of employee engagement. *Industrial & Organizational Psychology, 1*(1), 3–30.

Maclellan, D., Lordly, D., & Gingras, J. (2011). Professional socialization in dietetics: A review of the literature. *Canadian Journal of Dietetic Practice & Research, 72*(1), 37–42.

Mael, F., & Jex, S. (2015). Workplace boredom: An integrative model of traditional and contemporary approaches. *Group & Organization Management, 40*(2), 131–159.

Manroop, L., Singh, P., & Ezzedeen, S. (2014). Human resource systems and ethical climates: A resource-based perspective. *Human Resource Management, 53*(5), 795–816.

Marcum, J. W. (2013). Engagement: A leadership imperative. *Journal of the Library Administration & Management Section, 9*(2), 19–27.

Martin, H. J. (2010). Workplace climate and peer support as determinants of training transfer. *Human Resource Development Quarterly, 21*(1), 87–104. doi:10.1002/hrdq.20038

Maslach, C., & Leiter, M. P. (2008). Early predictors of job burnout and engagement. *Journal of Applied Psychology, 93*(3), 498–512.

Maslach, C., Schaufeli, W. B., & Leiter, M. P. (2001). Job burnout. *Annual Review of Psychology, 52,* 397–422.

Matthews, R. A., Mills, M. J., Trout, R. C., & English, L. (2014). Family-supportive supervisor behaviors, work engagement, and subjective well-being: A contextually dependent mediated process. *Journal of Occupational Health Psychology, 19*(2), 168–181, 14 p. doi:10.1037/a0036012

McAbee, S. L., & Graham, J. (2005). Expectations, realities, and perceptions of subject specialist librarians' duties in medium-sized academic libraries. *Journal of Academic Librarianship, 31*(1), 19–28.

McKay, R. (2015). Understanding and managing the anxiety surrounding performance evaluations: Considerations for the supervising librarian. *Library Leadership & Management, 29*(3), 1–11.

McKay, R., Arnold, D., Fratzl, J., & Thomas, R. (2008). Workplace bullying in academia: A Canadian study. *Employee Responsibilities & Rights Journal, 20*(2), 77–100.

Menguc, B., Auh, S., Fisher, M., & Haddad, A. (2013). To be engaged or not to be engaged: The antecedents and consequences of service employee engagement. *Journal of Business Research, 66,* 2163–2170.

Meyer, J. P., & Allen, N. J. (1991). A three-component conceptualization of organizational commitment. *Human Resource Management Review, 1*(1), 61.

Michaelson, C., Pratt, M. G., Grant, A. M., & Dunn, C. P. (2014). Meaningful work: Connecting business ethics and organization studies. *Journal of Business Ethics, 121*(1), 77–90.

Mishra, K., Boynton, L., & Mishra, A. (2014). Driving employee engagement: The expanded role of internal communications. *International Journal of Business Communication, 51*(2), 183–202.

Mitchell, J. I., Gagné, M., Beaudry, A., & Dyer, L. (2012). The role of perceived organizational support, distributive justice and motivation in reactions to new information technology. *Computers in Human Behavior, 28,* 729–738.

Modern Survey. (2015). *Employee engagement and unions.* Retrieved May 14, 2016, from http://www.modernsurvey.com/wp-content/uploads/2015/09/Employee-Engagement-and-Unions-Report.pdf

Morgan, C. (2014). Craft and librarianship: A reconsideration of the sources of librarian job satisfaction. *Journal of Library Administration, 54*(8), 637–658.

Motin, S. H. (2009). Bullying or mobbing: Is it happening in your academic library? *ACRL 14th National Conference Proceedings,* Chicago, IL: Association for College and Research Libraries, 291–297.

Mozenter, F. L., & Stickell, L. (2009). Without merit: One library's attempt to put "Merit" back in "Merit pay." *College & Research Libraries, 70*(1), 34–56.

Mylrea, M. F., Sen Gupta, T., & Glass, B. D. (2015). Professionalization in pharmacy education as a matter of identity. *American Journal of Pharmaceutical Education, 79*(9), 1–9.

Neary, S. (2014). Reclaiming professional identity through postgraduate professional development: Careers practitioners reclaiming their professional selves. *British Journal of Guidance & Counselling, 42*(2), 199–210.

Nikravan, L., & Frauenheim, E. (2014). Two years later . . . Still stressed & pressed. *Workforce, 93*(3), 35–37.

Olafsen, A. H., Halvari, H., Forest, J., & Deci, E. L. (2015). Show them the money? The role of pay, managerial need support, and justice in a self-determination theory model of intrinsic work motivation. *Scandinavian Journal of Psychology, 56*(4), 447–457.

Ollendorff, M. (1990). How much do librarians know about stress management? *Behavioral & Social Sciences Librarian, 8*(1), 67–98.

Organ, D. W. (1997). Organizational citizenship behavior: It's construct clean-up time. *Human Performance, 10*(2), 85.

Osawa, S. (2011). Workplace democracy and distributive justice: On the place of distributive principles of justice in the arguments for workplace democracy. *Journal of Political Science & Sociology, 15*(9), 51–70.

Patient, D. L., & Skarlicki, D. P. (2010). Increasing interpersonal and informational justice when communicating negative news: The role of the manager's empathic concern and moral development. *Journal of Management, 36*(2), 555.

Patillo, E., Moran, B. B., & Morgan, J. C. (2009). The job itself: The effects of functional units on work autonomy among public and academic librarians. *Library Trends,* (2), 276.

Pavlish, C., & Hunt, R. (2012). An exploratory study about meaningful work in acute care nursing. *Nursing Forum, 47*(2), 113–122.

Payne, S. C., & Webber, S. S. (2006). Effects of service provider attitudes and employment status on citizenship behaviors and customers' attitudes and loyalty behavior. *Journal of Applied Psychology, 91*(2), 365–378.

Peng, Y., Hwang, S., & Wong, J. (2010). How to inspire university librarians to become "Good soldiers"? The role of job autonomy. *The Journal of Academic Librarianship, 36*(4), 287–295.

Phillips, L. (2006). Work and be happy. *People Management, 12*(22), 17.

Podsakoff, N. P., Whiting, S. W., Podsakoff, P. M., & Blume, B. D. (2009). Individual- and organizational-level consequences of organizational citizenship behaviors: A meta-analysis. *Journal of Applied Psychology, 94*(1), 122–141.

Popova-Nowak, I. V. (n.d.). Work identity and work engagement. Retrieved from http://www.ufhrd.co.uk/wordpress/wp-content/uploads/2010/08/9_5.pdf

Prebble, M. (2016). Has the study of public service motivation addressed the issues that motivated the study? *American Review of Public Administration, 46*(3), 267–291.

Randhawa, G., & Kaur, K. (2015). An empirical assessment of impact of organizational climate on organizational citizenship behaviour. *Paradigm (09718907), 19*(1), 65–78.

Rees, C., Alfes, K., & Gatenby, M. (2013). Employee voice and engagement: Connections and consequences. *International Journal of Human Resource Management*, 24(14), 2780–2798.

Rich, B. L., Lepine, J. A., & Crawford, E. R. (2010). Job engagement: Antecedents and effects on job performance. *Academy of Management Journal*, 53(3), 617–635.

Robinson, K., Kennedy, N., & Harmon, D. (2012). Happiness: A review of evidence relevant to occupational science. *Journal of Occupational Science*, 19(2), 150–164. doi:10.1080/14427591.2011.634780

Rousseau, D. M. (1995). *Psychological contracts in organizations: Understanding written and unwritten agreements*. Thousand Oaks, CA: SAGE Publications.

Rousseau, D. M. (2001). Schema, promise and mutuality: The building blocks of the psychological contract. *Journal of Occupational & Organizational Psychology*, 74(4), 511–541.

Rousseau, D. M. (2003). Extending the psychology of the psychological contract—A reply to "putting psychology back into psychological contracts." *Journal of Management Inquiry*, 12(Part 3), 229–238.

Ryan, R. M., & Deci, E. L. (2000). Regular article: Intrinsic and extrinsic motivations: Classic definitions and new directions. *Contemporary Educational Psychology*, 25, 54–67.

Saddiq, S., & Burke, E. (2006). An investigation into the role of perceived work stress upon absenteeism, job satisfaction, psychological health and family, across 5 disparate occupational groups. Retrieved from http://www.distancelearningcentre.com/access/materials_old/hbs3/Perceived_work_stress.pdf

Saks, A. M. (2006). Antecedents and consequences of employee engagement. *Journal of Managerial Psychology*, 21(7), 600–619.

Saks, A. M., & Gruman, J. A. (2011). Getting newcomers engaged: The role of socialization tactics. *Journal of Managerial Psychology*, 26(5), 383–402.

Schaufeli, W. B., Salanova, M., Gonzalez-Roma, V., & Bakker, A. B. (2002). The measurement of engagement and burnout: A two sample confirmatory factor analytic approach. *Journal of Happiness Studies*, 3(1), 71–92.

Schmidt, S., Roesler, U., Kusserow, T., & Rau, R. (2014). Uncertainty in the workplace: Examining role ambiguity and role conflict, and their link to depression—A meta-analysis. *European Journal of Work & Organizational Psychology*, 23(1), 91–106.

Schneider, B. Ehrhart, M. G., & Macey, W. H. (2013). Organizational climate and culture. *Annual Review of Psychology*, 64, 361–388.

Schulte, P. A., Guerin, R. J., Schill, A. L., Bhattacharya, A., Cunningham, T. R., Pandalai, S. P., … Stephenson, C. M. (2015). Considerations for incorporating "well-being" in public policy for workers and workplaces. *American Journal of Public Health*, 105(8), e31.

Schwartz, M. (2016). Top skills for tomorrow's librarians: Library leaders share core competencies they'll be looking for over the next two decades—Some new, many familiar, but taken to the next level. *Library Journal*, 141(4), 38.

Sears, L. E., Shi, Y. Y., Coberley, C. R., & Pope, J. E. (2013). Overall well-being as a predictor of health care, productivity, and retention outcomes in a large employer. *Population Health Management*, 16(6), 397–405.

Shanock, L. R., & Eisenberger, R. (2006). When supervisors feel supported: Relationships with subordinates' perceived supervisor support, perceived organizational support, and performance. *Journal of Applied Psychology*, *91*(3), 689–695.

Shantz, A., Alfes, K., & Arevshatian, L. (2016). HRM in healthcare: The role of work engagement. *Personnel Review*, *45*(2), 274.

Shantz, A., Alfes, K., Truss, C., & Soane, E. (2013). The role of employee engagement in the relationship between job design and task performance, citizenship and deviant behaviours. *International Journal of Human Resource Management*, *24*(13), 2608–2627.

Sharif, M., & Scandura, T. (2014). Do perceptions of ethical conduct matter during organizational change? Ethical leadership and employee involvement. *Journal of Business Ethics*, *124*(2), 185–196.

Sheesley, D. F. (2001). Burnout and the academic teaching librarian: An examination of the problem and suggested solutions. *Journal of Academic Librarianship*, *27*(6), 447–451.

Shimazu, A., Schaufeli, W., Kamiyama, K., & Kawakami, N. (2015). Workaholism vs. work engagement: the two different predictors of future well-being and performance. *International Journal of Behavioral Medicine*, *22*(1), 18–23.

Shin, J., Seo, M., Shapiro, D. L., & Taylor, M. S. (2015). Maintaining employees' commitment to organizational change: The role of leaders' informational justice and transformational leadership. *Journal of Applied Behavioral Science*, *51*(4), 501.

Shoss, M. K., Eisenberger, R., Restubog, S. L., & Zagenczyk, T. J. (2013). Blaming the organization for abusive supervision: The roles of perceived organizational support and supervisor's organizational embodiment. *Journal of Applied Psychology*, *98*(1), 158–168.

Shuck, B., Collins, J. C., Rocco, T. S., & Diaz, R. (2016). Deconstructing the privilege and power of employee engagement. *Human Resource Development Review*, *15*(2), 208.

Shupe, E. I., Wambaugh, S. K., & Bramble, R. J. (2015). Role-related stress experienced by academic librarians. *Journal of Academic Librarianship*, *41*(3), 264–269.

Singh, R. (2016). The impact of intrinsic and extrinsic motivators on employee engagement in information organizations. *Journal of Education for Library & Information Science*, *57*(2), 197–206.

Smollan, R. K. (2016). The personal costs of organizational change: A qualitative study. *Public Performance & Management Review*, *39*(1), 223.

Srikanth, P. B., & Jomon, M. G. (2013). Role ambiguity and role performance effectiveness: Moderating the effect of feedback seeking behaviour. *Asian Academy of Management Journal*, *18*(2), 105–127.

Stead, B. A., & Scamell, R. W. (1980). A study of the relationship of role conflict, the need for role clarity, and job satisfaction for professional librarians. *Library Quarterly*, *50*, 310–323.

Sutherland, L., & Markauskaite, L. (2012). Examining the role of authenticity in supporting the development of professional identity: An example from teacher education. *Higher Education*, *64*(6), 747–766.

Thapisa, A. P. N. (1992). Work, its significance, meaning and challenges among library assistants. *Journal of Library Administration*, *16*(4), 19–43.

Tinney, M. (2015). Be well and prosper: Participation in corporate wellness pro-
    grams is waning, but four changes could lead to more employee involvement.
    TD Magazine, 69(6), 62.
Truss, C., Shantz, A., Soane, E., Alfes, K., & Delbridge, R. (2013). Employee
    engagement, organisational performance and individual well-being: Exploring
    the evidence, developing the theory. *The International Journal of Human
    Resource Management, 24*(14), 2657–2669.
Tvedt, S. D., Saksvik, P. O., & Nytrø, K. (2009). Does change process healthiness
    reduce the negative effects of organizational change on the psychosocial work
    environment? *Work & Stress, 23*(1), 80–98.
Van Yperen, N. W., Wörtler, B., & De Jonge, K. M. M. (2016). Full length article:
    Workers' intrinsic work motivation when job demands are high: The role of
    need for autonomy and perceived opportunity for blended working.
    Computers in Human Behavior, 60, 179–184.
Vries, G., Jehn, K., & Terwel, B. (2012). When employees stop talking and start
    fighting: The detrimental effects of pseudo voice in organizations. *Journal of
    Business Ethics, 105*(2), 221–230.
Warrner, J., Sommers, K., Zappa, M., & Thornlow, D. (2016). Decreasing work-
    place incivility *Nursing Management, 47*(1), 22.
Wheeler, R. (2014). Stereotype threat and law librarianship. *Law Library Journal,
    106*(3), 483–490.
White, H. S. (1990). Librarian burnout. *Library Journal, 115*(5), 64–65.
Wilkins Jordan, M. (2014). All stressed out, but does anyone notice? Stressors affect-
    ing public libraries. *Journal of Library Administration, 54*(4), 291–307.
Wilkinson, Z. T. (2015). A human resources dilemma? Emergent themes in the expe-
    riences of part-time librarians. *Journal of Library Administration, 55*(5), 343.
Wilson, K. M., & Halpin, E. (2006). Convergence and professional identity in the
    academic library. *Journal of Librarianship and Information Science, 38*(2),
    79–91.
Yalabik, Z. Y., van Rossenberg, Y., Kinnie, N., & Swart, J. (2015). Engaged and
    committed? The relationship between work engagement and commitment in
    professional service firms. *International Journal of Human Resource
    Management, 26*(12), 1602–1621.
Yu-Ping, P. (2012). The relationship between job satisfaction, job autonomy and job
    performance in university librarians. *Journal of Educational Media & Library
    Sciences, 49*(4), 563.

Index

Qualifications, 93, 99

Realistic job preview, 96
Recruitment, 22, 41, 63, 78, 82,
    83–84
Resistance to change, xx, 41, 109
Respect, 24, 26, 29, 35, 51, 95
Reward systems, 23, 29, 72, 81, 82,
    84–87, 106
Rewards, 21–23, 31
Role ambiguity, 3, 9, 11, 41, 48,
    66, 76; burnout and, xxii, 11; change
    and, 9
Role clarity, 30, 47–51, 91, 108, 109,
    113
Role conflict, 48; burnout and, xxii, 11;
    goals and, 3; psychological contract
    and, 11
Role confusion, 42
Role discrepancy, xvi
Role expansion, 41, 88
Role models, 93, 94, 112, 113

Satisfaction, Job. See Job satisfaction
Self-efficacy, 43, 79
Self-esteem, 42
Silos, 87
Socialization, professional, 6, 95
Spillover effect, 5, 7, 11, 13, 57, 62;
    customer service and, 65; well-being
    and, 67, 69
Sportsmanship and organizational
    citizenship behavior, 62
Status goals, 56, 58
Stereotype, 93, 99
Stress, 10, 30, 43, 66, 76; causes, 40,
    41, 50, 76, 88, 93, 97, 108;
    organizational change and, 13–14,
    109; supervisors and, 14
Stress management, 12, 41, 69
Substance abuse, xxii, 67
Supervision, 39

Supervisor behavior, 21, 39, 43, 44, 47,
    74. See also Manager behavior
Supervisor role, 75–76, 77, 78, 86
Supervisor support, 64, 69; emotional
    labor and, 9
Supervisor training, 49, 86
Support staff, 23, 38

Teamwork, 23, 36, 38, 105, 107;
    cross-functional, 87
Technological change, xxv; burnout
    and, xxiii
Tenure, 29
Training, 43, 75, 78–79. See also
    Learning and development
Training programs, 91, 93–97
Transformational leadership, 76, 86
Trust, 30, 74, 76, 103, 107, 112
Turnover, xxii

Unfairness. See Organizational Justice
Unions, 91, 99–101; distributive justice
    and, 21; procedural justice and, 19
User needs, 38

Values: personal, 78, 80, 82, 86, 98;
    professional, 6, 73, 92, 93, 94
Values, organizational, 78, 84, 92, 97,
    103; meaningfulness and, 33, 37, 38,
    73; recruitment and, 83; supervisor's
    role and, 75
Vision, organizational, 37, 68

Well-being, 42, 56, 66–69, 97
Work environment, 39
Work-life balance, 46, 88
Workload, 64, 79, 107; boredom and,
    xxiii–xxiv; burnout and, 11; change
    and, 14; supervisor workload, 40
Workplace culture, 2, 17, 33, 81
Workplace climate. See Organizational
    culture

About the Author

MARGARET ZELMAN LAW is a researcher, writer and frequent speaker in a variety of areas related to the management of libraries. After a career in management in public and academic libraries and library consortia, she began consulting with libraries in areas of organizational development, human resource issues and strategy. She contributes to global library development by volunteering as a trainer for libraries in developing countries. She is also an instructor at the School of Library and Information Studies, University of Alberta. In addition to a Master of Information Studies, from the University of British Columbia, she holds a Master of Business Administration and a Doctor of Business Administration. This book arose from her doctoral dissertation. Margaret Law lives in Edmonton, Alberta, and travels widely to work with libraries. She can be contacted at mzelmanlaw@gmail.com